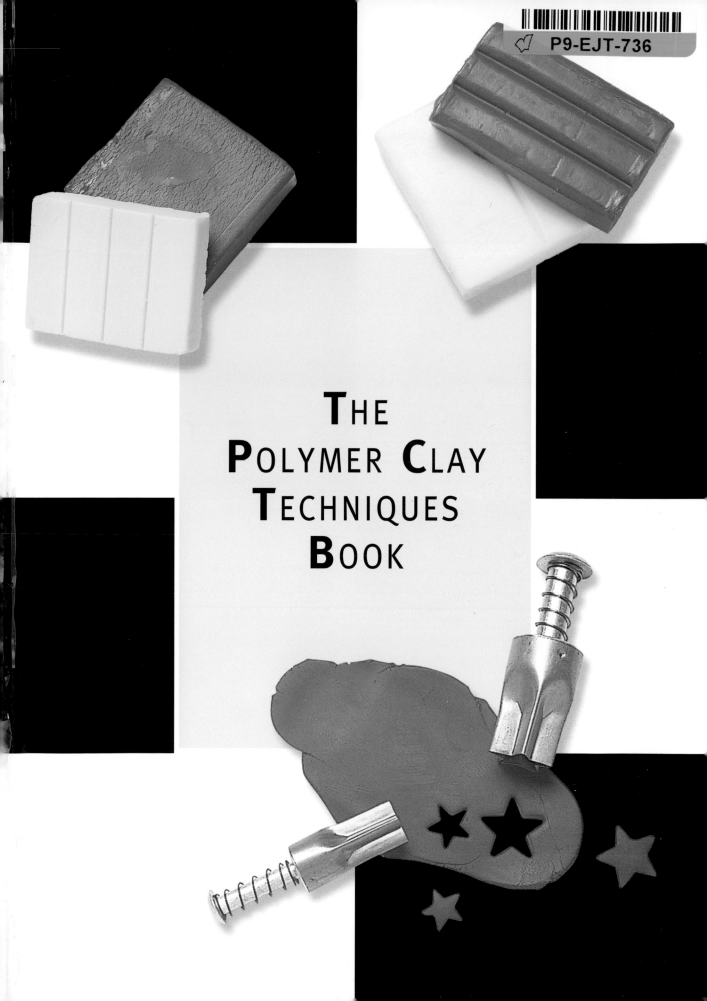

THE
POLYMER CLAY
TECHNIQUES
BOOK

THE
POLYMER CLAY
TECHNIQUES
BOOK

SUE HEASER

NORTH LIGHT BOOKS
Cincinnati, Ohio

A QUARTO BOOK

First published in North America by
North Light Books,
an imprint of F+W Publications, Inc.
4700 East Galbraith Road
Cincinnati, Ohio 45236
1-800/289-0963

ISBN-13: 978-1-58180-008-1
ISBN-10: 1-58180-008-8

Reprinted 2000 (twice), 2001, 2002, 2003,

2004 (twice), 2005, 2006, 2008

QUAR.LNK

Conceived, designed and produced by:
Quarto Publishing plc
The Old Brewery
6 Blundell Street
London N7 9BH

Editor: Sarah Vickery
Art editor: Francis Cawley
Assistant art director: Penny Cobb
Designer: Tanya Devonshire-Jones
Photographers: Pat Athie,
                        Colin Bowling
Illustrator: Jenny Dooge
Indexer: Dawn Butcher

Art director: Moira Clinch
Publisher: Piers Spence

Manufactured in Hong Kong by
Regent Publishing Services Ltd.

Printed in China by
SNP Leefung Printing Limited.

CONTENTS

INSPIRATION

Polymer clay is surely one of the most exciting new art materials of our time. Available in a glorious range of colors, it is a fine textured plastic modeling compound that can be baked to a permanent hardness in an ordinary home oven. This simple fact makes it an art medium that is accessible to everyone—there is no need for major outlay on a kiln or expensive tools.

For many years, polymer clay was largely used only by specialist modelers, or was seen as a child's toy. However, during the 1980s and 1990s, many gifted artists from all round the world discovered its extraordinary versatility and it is rapidly becoming an art medium in its own right. The range of artists who now use polymer clay is enormous: jewelers, sculptors, fine doll artists, miniaturists, illustrators, and animators are all recognizing it as a versatile material that gives techniques and results never before obtainable.

PATRICIA KIMLE
DECORATED EGGS
Canework, mokumé gané, and translucent layers decorate a glorious collection of hens' eggs in subtle color schemes.

CAROL BULL
WITH A PINT AND A SONG
Two gentlemen, slightly the worse for beer, are in mid song when Ma arrives... Superb polymer clay character sculpture with fabric clothes at the miniature scale of 1:12.

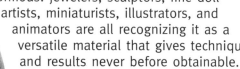

But it is not only in the professional and fine art world that polymer clay is being hailed as the art material of the 21st century. Home crafters and hobbyists everywhere are discovering the wonderful appeal and accessibility of this medium, particularly as it combines so well with other popular crafts, such as needlework, dollhouses and miniatures, painting, sculpture, and making gifts and jewelry.

If you are a beginner, this book gives you all the information you need to begin working with polymer clay and then go on to achieve increasingly advanced creations. If you are a seasoned polymer clay enthusiast, you will find a wonderful array of advanced methods here to tempt you. I hope that beginners and advanced 'polyclayers' alike will draw as much enjoyment from all these glorious techniques as I have.

AMELIA HELM
FACE STUDY
This striking image is created in polymer clay mosaic. The flowing lines of the tiles, or tesserae, enhance the superb three-dimensional effect.

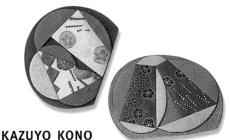

KAZUYO KONO
TWO BROOCHES
Caned plum blossoms decorate the pure lines of these stylish Japanese brooches. Metallic clays and geometric motifs add to the impact.

MARIE SEGAL
NECKLACE AND EARRINGS
Jewel-like miniature cane slices in the form of flowers, fruit, and even tiny teapots are used to create enchanting pieces of jewelry. Copper wire and metal findings add the finishing touches.

JODY BISHEL
GOLD ENAMEL PINS
Textured gold clay is highlighted with gold powders and then coated with layers of liquid polymer clay to make these glorious pins.

SUE HEASER
PIETRA DURA BOX
Convolvulus is a typical motif of 16th century Florentine pietre dure and is reproduced in this exquisite polymer clay version. A simple black box is an ideal mount for the flowing design.

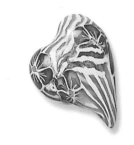

MARIE SEGAL
BEADS
The artist has attained an extraordinary quality of depth in these beads, which are virtually indistinguishable from lampwork glass beads. Foils and translucent caning effects simulate dichroic glass.

SUE HEASER
MINIATURE POT PLANTS
Polymer clay's fine texture is used to
advantage here to sculpt a variety of
plants only ¼ in (20mm) high.

HEN SCOTT
MOKUMÉ GANÉ PAPERWEIGHT
The finish on this paperweight vies with the
quality of Venetian glass. Translucent clays
are combined with silver leaf in a superb
variation of the mokumé gané technique.

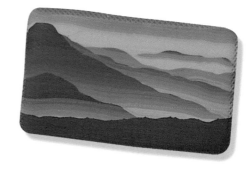

MIKE BUESSELER
LANDSCAPE PIN
This superb landscape cane was
inspired by the artist's home state
of Alaska.

SUE HEASER
MILLEFIORE BOTTLE
Colorful millefiore flower canes
cover a small glass bottle to make
an eye-catching and unusual
perfume bottle.

EQUIPMENT AND MATERIALS

EQUIPMENT

The basic equipment needed for working with polymer clay is simple and inexpensive. You will probably be able to find everything that you need in your home. The basic equipment is listed here, while more specialist tools and equipment for particular techniques are listed with the techniques themselves.

Work surface

A smooth work surface is essential. Many techniques require a surface that the clay can be stuck lightly to, so the surface needs to be smooth and shiny to allow this. A melamine chopping board, a ceramic tile, or a sheet of glass with the edges sanded are all excellent surfaces. The glass allows you to place graph paper under it for easy measuring. A ceramic tile can be used to place delicate pieces straight into the oven.

Cutting tools

Craft knife (Exacto): you will need a basic craft knife for cutting clay from the block and chopping lengths from logs. However, the craft knife is also a valuable applying tool and I find the curved blade shown in the photograph to be the most versatile. Blades: these are used for slicing millefiori canes and cutting straight edges. Tissue blades, which are long straight blades with a single cutting edge, are the most versatile and can be obtained from specialist polymer clay retailers. Razor blades or wallpaper scraper blades can be used instead and are readily available. To protect your fingers, bake a log of clay along one edge of two-edged razor blades. Ripple blades are used for exotic effects.

Sculpting tools

Besides tapestry needles, I use paintbrush handles, cocktail sticks, and even glass ball-headed pins for sculpting. You can purchase all kinds of branded sculpting and dental tools but I have never found them essential. Stainless steel works best for smoothing the surface of the clay.

PASTA MACHINES
These are invaluable for rolling out even clay sheets of various thicknesses, and can be used to mix and knead the clay as well.

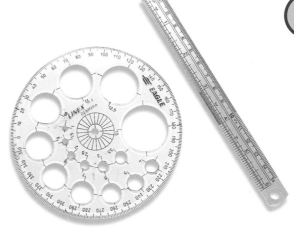
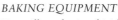

BAKING EQUIPMENT
You will need a (cookie) baking sheet lined with paper or baking parchment for baking your polymer clay creations.

Rolling tools

You will need a smooth rolling pin to roll out sheets of clay, and either a glass bottle or sturdy drinking glass is perfect for this. A perspex tube or a printer's brayer can also be used. For miniatures and smaller rollings, use a small bottle or a cake decorator's rolling pin. Pasta machines are a great aid to millefiori and when working with clay sheets.

Needle tools

I use a collection of different sizes of ordinary sewing and darning needles for piercing beads and making holes in the clay. Large tapestry or wool needles are my favorite tools and are useful for smoothing and sculpting the clay as well. You can mount needles in a polymer clay log and bake them to make a handle. A dried-up ballpoint pen refill is a useful tool for making larger holes.

Measuring tools

A small ruler is necessary for measuring the size of clay balls and logs. A draftsman's circle template is useful for measuring ball sizes.

Making your own tools

You can use the clay itself to make a variety of tools. Baked logs can be cut in half to give circular impressing tools. Stamps and texture tools can all be made from the clay, and suggestions for this are given in the techniques. The end of a paperclip can be hammered flat to make a tiny chisel and then given a clay handle.

MATERIALS

Polymer clay

Polymer clay is a fabulous material and it is only relatively recently that the art world has become fully aware of its potential. It can be used for more applications than virtually any other art medium and in genres as varied as textiles, sculpting, jewelry, doll-making, model-making, animation, and fine art.

Polymer clay is basically a plastic material and consists of PVC particles and pigment suspended in a plasticizer. This gives the clay its maleable consistency and the minute size of the plastic particles means that the clay has a very fine textured. Baking the clay evaporates the plasticizer and causes the particles to fuse together into a stable material.

Liquid polymer clay

This can be used for coating the solid clays to give glaze effects. It is available as both opaque and translucent liquid clay.

Clay softeners

Some manufacturers supply mixing agents for their clays. These can be mixed with the clay to soften it.

Leafs and foils

True gold leaf is extremely expensive but imitation leaf, or Dutch leaf, works beautifully in its place. It is available in variegated colors, as well as gold, silver, and copper. Plastic-backed metallic sheets of foil can be applied by pressing them onto a soft clay sheet, scraping them firmly on the back, and then ripping off the backing. They are available in many metallic colors, including holographic gold and silver.

The main brands of polymer clay all have the following properties:

- *The clay is fine-textured and can be modeled, sculpted, molded, sliced, grated, rolled into sheets, and extruded*
- *The clay surface can be stamped, textured, and coated with powders colors and metallic leafs*
- *It can be mixed with a variety of inclusions to give added textures and effects*
- *It is available in a wide range of colors that are mixable to produce an even larger palette*
- *The clay remains soft until baked, and unbaked clay has a shelf life of several years. It will, however, become harder as time passes*
- *The baked clay is slightly flexible and robust, although the strength varies between brands*
- *There is virtually no shrinkage or color change on baking and the baked clay lasts indefinitely*
- *Once baked it can be carved, sawn, cut, drilled, glued, painted, sanded, and buffed*
- *Baked clay can have fresh clay added to it and then be re-baked many times*

Page 125 lists the main brands available and their various properties.

Varnishes

Always use either alcohol-based (spirit-based) or water-based varnishes with polymer clay. Avoid enamel or oil-based varnishes, which will never dry properly. The manufacturers supply their own gloss and matt varnishes, or you can use artist's acrylic mediums.

PAINTS
Acrylic paints are the
best kind to use
on polymer
clay.
Do not use
enamel paint, which will never dry completely. Artist's
acrylic paints are ideal, as are any good quality craft
acrylic paint.

Glues

It is important to choose the right kind of glue:

- *Two-part epoxy glue is recommended for gluing metal jewelry findings to baked clay. The slower setting kind is the strongest.*
- *Superglues are available in both gel and liquid forms. Use them to glue baked clay to baked clay to provide a very strong bond.*
- *PVA glue is the white craft glue that is plastic-based. It can be used to glue fabric and dolls' hair to baked polymer clay. Brush onto baked clay, glass, or ceramics to provide a key for applying fresh clay.*
- *Stick glues for gluing paper and card can be used to smear onto baked clay to provide a key for adding soft clay.*

STORING POLYMER CLAY

Polymer clay does not dry out and has a long shelf life, although it will become harder with time. You can extend the shelf life of your clay if you follow a few simple rules:

- *Store clay in a cool place away from heat and sunlight.*
- *Opened packs of clay will not dry out, but it is best to keep them away from dust in an airtight container such as a tin.*
- *Polymer clay will react with some types of plastic so do not store it in plastic containers unless it is wrapped.*
- *Do not wrap polymer clay in paper or the plasticizer will leach out. Use baking parchment or polythene bags.*

Powders

Powder colors can be brushed onto the soft clay before baking, where they will cling to create many beautiful effects. Brush powders onto the unbaked clay with a soft paintbrush or your fingertip. Avoid using cosmetic powders as they can be unpredictable and will discolor in time.

- *Metallic powders are available in many different colors, as well as pearl and interference shades.*
- *Artist's soft pastels are long lasting and come in*

hundreds of colors. Pastels work best when applied to paler clay colors, as they may not be visible on dark clay. To apply artist's pastel, simply rub the color onto some scrap paper to produce powder. The color can be applied to either soft or baked clay, although more subtle effects are gained from working with baked clay.

- *Embossing powders are useful for mixing into the clay for simulating stone effects, as well as for applying to the clay surface. They are widely available from rubber stamp suppliers.*
- *Glitter can be mixed with the clay or brushed on.*

Getting Started: Basic Techniques

This model car with turning wheels is made entirely with polymer clay: even complex models use simple shapes of logs, balls, and sheets.

WORK AREA

Polymer clay is a very undemanding medium when it comes to somewhere to work. You can use a kitchen or dining room table, a desk, or even a tray on your lap for some projects. However, if you spend considerable time working with the clays, you will want to make yourself more comfortable and, ideally, create a permanent area for your work. A sturdy table that will not wobble when you roll out clay is

GENERAL TIPS

- *Keep your hands clean and wash or wipe them with wet wipes between colors.*
- *Keep your fingernails reasonably short.*
- *Do not push and poke at the clay when applying pieces; it is better to remove a piece you do not like and re-apply, to attain a professional result.*
- *Save all your scrap clay—it can be mixed to make a gray that can then be used in many ways.*

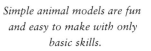

Simple animal models are fun and easy to make with only basic skills.

Measuring

All step-by-step demonstrations give measurements to help you to keep to the right size. The diameter of balls is given, the thickness and length of logs, and the thickness of sheets. To measure the sizes, you can use a ruler laid on your work surface, or you can make a card template. Use a piece of stiff card and cut out notches of different measurements along the edges. Each notch should be slightly deeper than it is long. You can then place the notches over balls and logs to check their size.

MAKING LOGS, BALLS, AND SHEETS

Working with polymer clay uses modeling skills that most of us learnt in childhood, making it an accessible craft to many people. The following steps will help you to hone these natural skills to the best advantage. Logs, balls, and sheets of clay are the basic shapes used in virtually every technique.

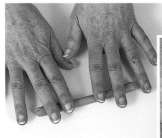

Making logs

1 Place a kneaded lump of clay on your work surface and shape it into a rough log by rolling it on the surface with your hand. Once the log has formed you can continue to make it longer and thinner by rolling with your fingers splayed out. Keep your fingers moving up and down the log to prevent any ridges or thin areas developing.

2 You can roll polymer clay into extremely thin logs of about $\frac{1}{32}$ in (1mm) or less. The best way to do this is to roll with the fingers of one hand while holding the end of the log with the other. Gently pull the thinner portion out and away as it forms.

essential, and you will need a chair that allows you to sit comfortably at the table. Plenty of space for your work surface, room to lay out the clays and tools, and somewhere to store equipment and partly finished projects will all add to your comfort.

KEEPING CLEAN

Polymer clay easily picks up dust, lint, and animal hair so you will need to keep your work area as clean as possible. Wipe the work surface before you start and cover it with a cloth or polythene sheet to protect when you are not working. Some clays will stain your hands more than others, and if you find this happening use wet wipes to clean your hands between colors.

KNEADING THE CLAY

There is much advice given about 'conditioning' polymer clay by kneading it for long periods of time to ensure that it is ready for use. However, the major manufacturers assure me that this is unnecessary and you should only knead the clay until it is soft and maleable. Some softer clays can even be used straight from the packet. If the clay is too soft, you can leach it to make it firmer. To do this, press a pancake of clay between two sheets of ordinary white paper and leave overnight. The plasticizer will be drawn out of the clay into the paper.

Clay that is old and hard can be chopped into small cubes and crushed with a rolling pin to soften it, or use a proprietary mixing agent.

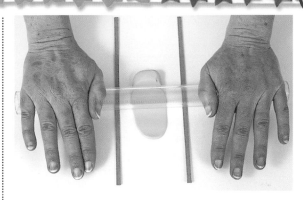

Making balls

1 Form a log of clay and cut a few lengths. Place one of these into your palm and cover it with the other palm. Rotate the top palm over the bottom palm, pressing down hard onto the clay at first and then more lightly. This will create a ball.

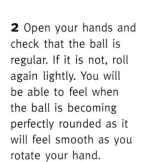

2 Open your hands and check that the ball is regular. If it is not, roll again lightly. You will be able to feel when the ball is becoming perfectly rounded as it will feel smooth as you rotate your hand.

A model penguin is made by pressing simple shapes of clay together.

Making sheets

Lay a log of clay on your work surface and place strips of card or wood on either side of the clay. Roll out the clay between the strips as though it is pastry, using your roller. When the roller reaches the strips, it will be prevented from rolling the clay too thin and you will be left with an even sheet.

A pasta machine is a wonderful tool for rolling out even clay sheets. Set the machine on the thickest setting. Flatten the clay in your hands until it is ¼ in (6mm) thick, and feed it into the top while you turn the handle. Adjust the machine's setting to roll it thinner.

COLOR MIXING

A rainbow of colors can be mixed from just three clay colors: magenta, blue, and yellow.

Most brands of polymer clay come in a large range of colors that can be mixed together to form even more shades. You can also mix your own palette from a few basic clay colors, although the brilliance of the mixtures will vary between the brands. This section gives you the basic information you need to mix colors for any technique.

When color mixtures are given in the instructions, they refer to how many parts of each color you will need to mix to make the new color. A simple way to measure parts is to roll a log of each color and cut them into the required number of equal lengths.

To make a green that requires three parts yellow and two parts blue, for example, roll equal thickness logs of yellow and blue. Cut three ½ in (13mm) lengths of yellow and two ½ in (13mm) lengths of blue. Roll these together into a log, then fold the log in half and roll again. The colors will become streaky and marbled. Continue folding and rolling until the colors merge together to form a solid green.

The photograph above shows the excellent color range that can be achieved by mixing just three different shades of polymer clay. The brand shown has particularly brilliant colors. For the most accurate color mixing, you will need clay colors that are closest to the colors of printing: magenta, cyan, and yellow. Use crimson, magenta, or a strong pink clay; a cobalt type of blue; and a lemon or zinc yellow. These three form the primary colors and are mixed to form the secondary colors of red orange (or scarlet), green, and purple. Adding white or translucent clay will give pastel colors, while adding black will give smoky shades.

Proportions of the different colors are given in the color mixtures. However, the intensity of pigments varies considerably between brands so you may need to adjust the quantities depending on the clay you are using.

RIGHT: Basic colors used in this book and available in most clay brands.

BELOW: Colors that can be mixed from the above colors. Many of these can be purchased as well.

1   2   3   4   5   6   7

8   9   10   11   12   13   14

15   16   17   18   19   20   21   22

COLORS USED IN THE TECHNIQUES

The various brands of polymer clays come in a wide range of colors but they vary from brand to brand. For this reason, I have used descriptive names for the colors in this book. Use the color closest to the one in the photograph.

MARBLING

Marbling is achieved by mixing two or more colors together until the clay is streaked. It is used for many lovely effects, ranging from simulated stone and wood grain to fantasy stripes and streaks.

Marbled clay has been used to make this potted vessel, giving wonderful swirls of color.

COLORS AVAILABLE IN MOST MAIN CLAY BRANDS:

1 *White*
2 *Black*
3 *Translucent*
4 *Magenta*
5 *Crimson*

6 *Red*
7 *Orange*
8 *Yellow*
9 *Green*
10 *Turquoise*

11 *Blue*
12 *Violet*
13 *Dark brown*
14 *Flesh*

THESE COLORS ALLOW YOU TO MIX:

15 *Beige = white + trace of brown*
16 *Ocher = brown + yellow + white*
17 *Golden yellow = yellow + trace of orange*
18 *Leaf green = 2 parts green + 1 part brown*
19 *Light brown = white + brown*
20 *Pink = white + trace of red or crimson*
21 *Gray = white + black*
22 *Burgundy = crimson + trace of black*
A pale or light version of any color can be mixed by adding a small quantity of the color to white or translucent clay. Pearly colors can be mixed by adding a little of the color to pearl.

SPECIALTY COLORS

Several brands also have the following specialty colors:
● *Metallic colors such as gold, silver, and copper*
● *Pearl white and pearlescent colors*
● *Stone effect clays with added inclusions*
● *Fluorescent colors*
● *Glow-in-the-dark clay*
● *Translucent colors*
● *Clays with added glitter*
Transparent or translucent clays are not glass clear, although very thin layers of these clays can be buffed to give glassy effects.

1 Form logs of the colors you wish to marble; this example shows pink, white, and blue. Twist the logs together and then roll them as one to make a larger log. Fold the log in half and roll again. Continue folding and rolling and the streaks will become finer each time. Stop before the streaks merge into a new color. Twisting the log after each fold will give more random swirls in the clay.

2 Marbled clay can be rolled into a sheet to be used for various purposes, and this shows off the marbled effect beautifully. Roll out the clay in the direction of the stripes for thinner, more regular effects. Roll across the stripes for broader and irregular bands. You can also feather the surface by drawing a point across the bands and rolling the surface again.

MAKING BLENDS

You can turn clay into a graduated sheet of color by using a simple process that is called the Skinner Blend after Judith Skinner, its inventor. This technique is particularly useful for millefiori but has many other applications as well.

GETTING STARTED

1 Roll out a sheet of pink clay and another of blue. Cut a triangle of each color and place them together on your work surface to form a rectangular sheet. Fold the sheet in half.

2 Roll out the sheet lengthways, or pass it through a pasta machine. The blue side of the clay is clearly visible opposite the pink side with a mixture of the colors appearing between.

3 Fold the sheet in half again, in the same way, and roll out lengthways. Continue folding in half and rolling, keeping the edges neat. You will find that the colors begin to blend in the central area.

4 After about 30 rollings, the clay will form a sheet that grades from pink, through violet, to blue. To turn it into a graded loaf, lay it on your work surface and fold it over about 1 in (25mm) from the end, fold again in the other direction, and work upwards in a concertina fashion.

5 To make a log that grades from one color in the center to another at the outside, simply roll the sheet up as shown. You can use this technique to make blends of many different colors. You can even make a rainbow blend using three colors, adding the third color as another triangle at one end.

Using Cutters and Clay Extruders

Polymer clay cuts beautifully with all forms of cookie or pastry cutters, canapé cutters, gum paste (sugar craft) cutters, and sandwich cutters. Metal cutters usually work best, having a sharper cutting edge than plastic cutters.

A simple clay extruder comes with a variety of plates and can be used to extrude polymer clay. However, it is only possible to use these with the softest clay brands—the force needed to extrude firm clay makes using the extruder a painful business! There are various solutions to this problem, such as adapting a caulking gun to give more leverage.

USING CUTTERS

1 Roll out the clay and brush over the surface sparingly with a paintbrush dipped in talcum powder to prevent the cutter sticking. Press the cutter down firmly.

2 To make a beveled or domed edge, cover the clay sheet with plastic film and press the cutter down. Remove the cutter and film, and cut through the clay.

USES FOR CUT-OUT CLAY SHAPES

- *As simple shapes for badges, pins, or pendants*
- *As jewelry blanks upon which to build more elaborate designs in clay*
- *For cutting out the basic shape of flowers and leaves before sculpting them into realistic shapes*
- *For cutting out repeat patterns for appliqué*
- *For stamping into the clay to make surface patterns*

USING A CLAY EXTRUDER

Knead the clay until it is as soft as possible, adding mixing medium or diluent depending on the brand. Press a walnut-sized lump into the extruder, insert the plunger and press hard to extrude the clay. You can change plates without emptying the extruder. To empty the clay from the extruder, remove the plate and press the plunger to push out the clay.

USES FOR EXTRUDED CLAY

- *Fine multi-hole plates will produce thin logs that can be made into hair for models*
- *Single-hole plates extrude logs with various cross sections that can be sliced to make shapes for decorating projects or making miniature food*

BAKING

Support thin clay forms, such as flowers, with foil while baking to prevent sagging.

Baking polymer clay is a very simple process but one that needs care. Most polymer clays bake at 275°F (130°C) but a few bake at 212°F (100°C), so check the packet first. Timings can also vary between the brands.

Baked polymer clay does not attain its full hardness until it has cooled. Even then, you will find it is slightly flexible, although the degree of flexibility varies between brands. Final strength also varies between brands so check the table on page 125 for details.

It is a good idea to test your oven before baking a project—home ovens often have inaccurate thermostats. To test, make several small balls of clay and press them together in pairs. Bake on a lined baking sheet at the

BAKING BEADS

As illustrated here, beads can be baked in various ways to prevent them rolling and spoiling: they can be threaded onto a wire or skewer and held across the top of a pan with pieces of scrap clay; placed in a piece of paper with concertina folds; or simply placed upright onto the paper lining of the pan. Any slight marks from where they rest will be invisible once the beads are strung.

BAKING SHEETS

When baking sheets of clay, you will need to keep them flattened with a weight to prevent warping or bubbling. Lay the sheet on a ceramic tile, cover with a piece of smooth paper or baking parchment, and place a second tile upside-down on top. Bake this sandwich for at least 10 minutes longer than usual because the tiles will insulate the clay from the heat.

BAKING TIPS

Thinner forms of clay are liable to sag in the heat of the oven before they harden. To prevent this, use pieces of foil to prop up clay shapes and keep them in position. Delicate pieces such as flowers can be hung from skewers inside jelly (jam) jars for baking.

recommended temperature and time given on the clay packet. When the clay is completely cool, check the balls and try to separate them. If they look shiny or discolored and are extremely hard to separate, the oven was too hot. If they separate easily without any sign of the two pieces fusing together, the oven was too cool. If separating the balls causes a slight tear, it was just right.

This baked box lid has been embellished with appliqué (see page 48) and baked again to give a cameo effect.

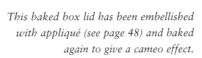

MULTIPLE BAKING

Polymer clay can be baked over and over again without any harm, as long as the normal baking temperature is not exceeded. This useful quality means that extremely complex projects can be built up by adding unbaked clay to baked clay and then re-baking many times.

It is sometimes difficult to make the soft clay stick to the baked clay—to overcome this problem, you need to give the fresh clay a key. This can either be stick glue, PVA glue, diluent, or liquid clay. It does not matter if the glue dries, as it will still provide a key.

Multiple baking can be used to delightful effect to make cameos. First, make a basic cabochon and bake it. When it is cool, smear the surface with a thin coat of stick glue. You can now apply a layer of contrasting clay and sculpt it into the cameo far more easily than if the cabochon had still been soft. The new clay will adhere well to the glue and, when baked again, will form a strong bond.

Multiple baking can be used to apply further shapes to a clay project that would be too fragile to add to when soft. Here, for example, a handle is added to a baked miniature jug. Use glue to give the soft clay a key.

CARVING, CUTTING, AND DRILLING BAKED CLAY

Baked polymer clay is not a particularly hard substance and can easily be carved, cut, sawn, filed, or drilled. The different brands vary as to how well they can be treated in this way, because some are more brittle than others. Be sure that you have baked the piece thoroughly, because under-baked clay is liable to be too brittle to carve or cut smoothly and may crumble. Warm clay is easier to cut or carve than cooled clay. Carved or cut lines in the baked clay will often have a white appearance that can be removed by re-baking the piece.

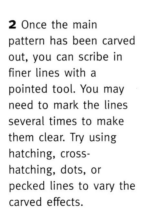

Carving

1 To carve motifs on baked polymer clay, first draw your design lightly with a soft pencil. Then use a lino cutter with a fine U-shaped cutter to gouge along the lines. It is best to cut lightly at first and then deepen the lines. Push the cutter away from you to make the best lines.

A simulated bone bead. The carved lines are accentuated with brown acrylic paint.

2 Once the main pattern has been carved out, you can scribe in finer lines with a pointed tool. You may need to mark the lines several times to make them clear. Try using hatching, cross-hatching, dots, or pecked lines to vary the carved effects.

Filing

Filing can be used to create incised decoration around a bead. The softness of baked polymer clay means that you will only need a few gentle strokes with the file to create quite deep cuts. You can mimic the effects of wheel-cut glass on the surfaces of beads and vessels with this technique.

Drilling

Polymer clay can be drilled successfully, a technique that can be used to enlarge the hole in a bead or make a hole after a piece has been baked. Simply twist a drill bit in the hole by hand to enlarge a bead hole, or make a hole in a thin piece of clay. If you need to drill through thick clay, you should use a small hobby drill and make a pilot hole first.

Sanding and Buffing

These two techniques have an almost magical effect on baked polymer clay. Sanding will smooth the clay, remove irregularities on the surface, and prepare the surface for buffing. Buffing then gives the clay a wonderful shine that resembles a glassy surface.

When translucent clays are buffed, their translucence is enhanced until any very thin layers become transparent.

Simulated rose quartz beads demonstrate the effects of sanding and buffing—only the right-hand bead has been treated.

Sanding

1 It is best to wet-sand polymer clay as this prevents the sandpaper becoming clogged with dust. Sand in a bowl of water or under a gently running tap. You will obtain the best effects if you first sand with coarser grits of wet and dry sandpaper, moving on to finer grits such as 800 or 1200 afterwards.

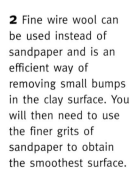

2 Fine wire wool can be used instead of sandpaper and is an efficient way of removing small bumps in the clay surface. You will then need to use the finer grits of sandpaper to obtain the smoothest surface.

Buffing

1 When the clay surface is sanded smooth, polish it hard with a piece of quilt wadding or stiff fabric to remove the tiny scratches left from the sanding and give the clay a wonderful sheen. This is particularly effective when creating simulated precious stones and metallic or translucent effects.

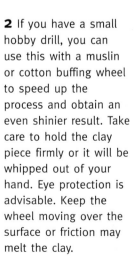

2 If you have a small hobby drill, you can use this with a muslin or cotton buffing wheel to speed up the process and obtain an even shinier result. Take care to hold the clay piece firmly or it will be whipped out of your hand. Eye protection is advisable. Keep the wheel moving over the surface or friction may melt the clay.

Gluing and Varnishing

Polymer clay can be glued very successfully although you must be careful only to use glues that are compatible with the clays (see page 125). When using epoxy glues, always swab the surfaces to be glued with denatured alcohol (methylated spirits) to remove any grease and ensure a strong bond.

Varnishing polymer clay is not normally necessary and varnish should only be used for specific purposes. Gloss varnish gives the clay a shiny surface suitable for jewelry or, in the case of miniatures, to simulate wet, shiny, or greasy surfaces. It can be used when buffing is not appropriate or desirable. Matt varnish is normally used to protect painted

GLUING CLAY TO METAL

1 Two-part epoxy glues are the best for gluing polymer clay to jewelry findings of all kinds. First squeeze out equal quantities of glue and hardener on some scrap card, and mix them thoroughly using a cocktail stick.

2 Apply the glue to the brooch pin and then press the pin firmly onto the back of the polymer clay piece. It is a good idea to use a sand tray to steady brooches while they set. The glue can take several hours to become firm—and up to 24 hours to set completely—so the brooch back may slide off unless it is held perfectly horizontal.

3 Wire mesh is useful for holding stud earrings horizontal while they are setting. Bend down the two ends of the mesh to make a raised surface for the stud posts to be pushed into.

GLUING CLAY TO CLAY

One of the branded superglues is the best to use for gluing baked polymer clay to baked polymer clay. The resulting bond is extremely strong and can be used for assembling polymer clay structures of all kinds, and for mending broken polymer clay pieces. Be careful when using these glues as they bond human flesh even better than polymer clay! After using any superglue, wipe the nozzle of the bottle and replace the cap.

surfaces on polymer clay when a shiny effect would not be appropriate, such as when painting sculpted faces.

Both types of varnish can be used to form a barrier on the clay before painting. Some clays can cause paint to bleed into the surrounding area after a period of time so varnishing is a wise precaution when painting features on faces or delicate patterns onto beads or miniature china.

Apply varnish sparingly with a soft brush. One coat is usually sufficient but if you want thicker varnish, it is better to apply several thin coats.

Complex models can be created with polymer clay by baking the parts separately and then assembling the model using a strong glue.

1 Squeeze out a small pool of glue onto a piece of foil. Dip a cocktail stick into the glue and apply to one of the surfaces. Here a thwart, or seat, is to be glued into a polymer clay model boat. The pool of glue will remain wet and usable for some time and this method gives you good control over the use of this type of glue.

2 Press the piece home and hold it there for a few moments. The bond will be almost instant so be sure that you have placed the piece accurately. If you make a mistake, you will need to cut the two pieces apart and start again. Wipe excess glue away with a tissue.

VARNISHING

1 To varnish a single large bead, push it onto a thick needle that is a tight fit in the hole so that the bead cannot rotate. You will be able to turn the bead as you brush on the varnish.

2 To varnish small beads, make a loop in one end of a length of wire as a stop and thread the beads onto the wire. Hold them tightly against the end loop so that they cannot rotate freely and paint on the varnish, turning the wire as necessary. If you also turn a hook in the other end of the wire, you can hang the beads up to dry.

3 Miniature crockery is difficult to varnish because the pieces are so tiny. The solution is to hold each piece down with a needle while you varnish.

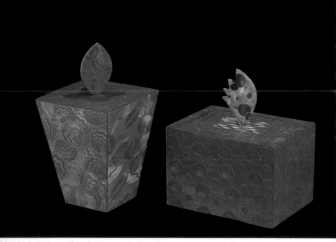

PIER VOULKOS & DANIEL PETERS
Veneered Boxes
Pier Voulkos developed these stunning gold and pearlescent clay effects. They are shown to perfection as veneers on Daniel Peter's Baltic birch wood boxes.

DIANE DUNVILLE
Mood Indigo Lamp
Layers of translucent clay were applied over Wireform mesh to create this beautiful lamp. Veneers of colored and translucent clay were then added along with texturing and carved details.

AKIKO KASE
Necklace
Caning, beads, and symbolic forms from several cultures are combined with sizzling colors to create this unique pendant necklace. Pure silk tassels finish the piece.

MARIE SEGAL
Complex Cane Slices
Many different caning techniques including blends, flowers, landscapes, and geometric designs are used to create these outstanding canes.

MIKE BUESSELER
LOCKET

Pearlescent clays give a rich dimension to this ingenious locket. Behind the tiny spiral door lies a glass heart bead.

AMELIA HELM
MOSAIC PANEL: RE/DISCOVERY

This sensitive image is created using soft polymer clay tiles. The sketched images are carved into the baked background clay and then back-filled with soft clay.

MANIPULATING THE CLAY

Polymer clay can be manipulated in an astonishing variety of ways and artists are constantly exploring new techniques.

CHRISTINE ALIBERT
MOSAIC VASE

Intricate mosaic canes with images of dolphins and key patterns are applied to a simple glass bottle. After baking, the surface is sanded and buffed to produce a stylish vase.

SYLVIA SCHMAHMANN
SEVEN SISTERS PIN

The same face cane is used for all the faces in this charming pin. Each sister has a different caned hairstyle, hat, and embellishments.

BEADS, BUTTONS, AND CABOCHONS

Polymer clay is a perfect material for making beads, buttons, and cabochons, and their simple shapes mean that even a beginner can achieve quality results. The bright colors of the clay and its ability to be mixed give a stunning palette from which finished pieces of virtually any color or color combination can be created. Many of the decorative techniques in this book can be applied to bead and button making for an extraordinary array of different types of jewelry.

These simple round beads have been decorated with millefiori cane slices.

YOU WILL NEED

- *Polymer clay in the color of your choice*
- *Darning needle*
- *Thick tapestry needle for larger beads*
- *Baking sheet lined with paper or baking parchment*
- *Bicone beads: a small tin lid or smooth tile*
- *Disc beads: a ceramic tile*
- *Tube beads: a metal knitting needle or wooden barbecue skewer*

ROUND BEADS

Simple round beads are the easiest to make and form the basis of many variations.

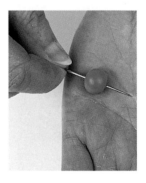

1 To make round beads that are all the same size, form a log of clay, about ½ in (13mm) thick and lay it onto a ruler. Cut along the ruler at ½ in (13mm) intervals to give even sized pieces of clay that will make ½ in (13mm) diameter beads. Lengths of ¼ in (6mm) long cut from a ¼ in (6mm) thick log will give ¼ in (6mm) diameter beads, and so on.

2 Roll each length into a ball. Using a sharp darning needle, pierce straight downwards into the center of one of the balls. This is easiest to do accurately if you hold your head directly over the bead. You will feel the needle stop as its point reaches the work surface.

3 Lift the bead on the needle and gently hold it on either side with thumb and forefinger. Twist the needle and push it further into the bead so that the bead is fully on the needle.

4 Roll the bead, still on the needle, back and forth on the side of your hand. This will make the bead rotate on the needle and enlarges the hole. It will also smooth the bead back into a ball shape if it was squashed slightly by being pierced. You can repeat, using a larger needle, if you want a larger hole. Do not touch the bead any more or you will distort it—just drop it off the needle onto the baking sheet and then use one of the methods given on page 20 for baking beads.

BEADS

A combination of simple round beads, discs, and melon beads creates a delicate necklace.

Bead making is one of our most ancient crafts—people have been creating beads from every available material since prehistoric times. Polymer clay is another material in this long line, and is probably one of the simplest to use. The following instructions will help you to make beads of many kinds, and show you how to achieve highly professional results.

The marvel of polymer clay is that while you can make simple beads of one color, you can also use an almost endless number of techniques to embellish your beads. Millefiori caning, metallic powders, stamping, molding, metal leaf, sculpting, painting—the list is enormous, and it is great fun to experiment.

MELON BEADS

These are sometimes called fluted beads, and look particularly effective when coated with metal powders and interspersed with colored beads.

Make a round bead and pierce it with the darning needle. While the bead is still on the darning needle, hold a thick tapestry needle alongside the bead, parallel with the darning needle, and press it against the side of the bead to indent it. Make similar, evenly spaced, indentations all round. The darning needle inside the bead will give you a firm surface to press against. Finish the bead by rolling on your palm as demonstrated in Round Beads.

DISC BEADS

These simple flat beads look best when strung between other types of beads as spacers and accents. They can be used on either side of a large bead to accent it, or to correct a hole that is too large.

1 Cut a log into equal lengths. You will need relatively small balls of clay to make these beads. Form small balls and press each one down onto a ceramic tile with the flat pad of your finger to make small discs. The more you press down, the larger they will become, but do not make them thinner than about 1/16 in (2mm). You should be able to keep them very round if you press down evenly.

2 Pierce the center of each bead with the darning needle and rotate it a little to enlarge the hole. Bake the beads on the tile, without moving them so that they do not distort. After baking, you can remove them from the tile.

BICONE BEADS

This is a traditional bead shape that looks like two cones placed together, and is very easy to make.

Make a round ball and place it on your work surface. Take a tin lid (or a small tile) with a smooth, flat surface and press it down onto the ball. Now rotate the tin lid in small circles, still holding it horizontally and pressing firmly down onto the ball. At first the movement will feel bumpy and then will become smooth. Lift up the tin lid and you will have a perfect bicone shape. Now pierce it through the points to make a bead.

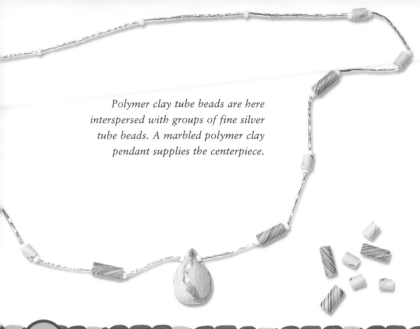

Polymer clay tube beads are here interspersed with groups of fine silver tube beads. A marbled polymer clay pendant supplies the centerpiece.

STRINGING BEADS

Stringing materials can be purchased from craft and hobby shops, as well as from specialist jewelry materials suppliers. Use cotton and silk cord, or a leather thong for large beads. Smaller beads are best threaded on beading thread or beading silk.

There is a wide variety of metal clasps and hooks available to give your necklaces a professional finish.

TUBE BEADS

This is another traditional shape of bead that can either be used as a single type in one necklace or combined with other bead shapes. To vary the size of the beads, vary the size of the knitting needle. For tiny tube beads, try rolling out the clay on a $\frac{1}{32}$ in (1mm) brass rod, available from hobby suppliers. This example uses marbled clay to give beads with a striped spiral design but you can, of course, use plain clay.

3 When the clay is about $\frac{1}{4}$ in (6mm) thick and forms an even log all along the needle, twist it gently round the needle so that the marbled stripes form a spiral. You can vary how much you twist to affect the angle of the spiral.

4 Bake the clay on the knitting needle for about 20 minutes, depending on the thickness of the log. When the clay has cooled enough to handle, but is still warm, cut the log into regular lengths, using a ruler as a guide. If the clay cools too much and you find it difficult to remove the needle, replace it in the oven to warm it.

1 Marble together purple and white clay until you have a log of striped clay. Pierce down through the center of the log with a knitting needle, keeping the needle central.

2 With the knitting needle still in the log, lay it on your work surface and roll gently to thin and extend it in either direction along the knitting needle. If the clay begins to pull away from the needle, squeeze it back onto the needle all along its length and continue.

These pendant drops have been painted with cave art images and threaded onto head pins to make an unusual pair of earrings.

The metallic beads are foil core beads, stamped and incised, then brushed with metallic powders (see page 90). The large foil core bead is carved, simulated bone.

PENDANT DROPS

These are an ideal shape for drop earrings and look particularly good made with a faux stone mixture, such as lapis lazuli or rose quartz.

Form a ball for a bead in the usual way and then roll the ball on your work surface, rolling mostly on one side of the ball to thin that side and elongate it. Pierce the bead down through its length with a darning needle and then roll lightly to correct any distortion from the piercing.

FOIL CORE BEADS

Wrapping clay around a ball of aluminum foil is a useful technique for making larger beads. The resulting beads are lighter than if made with solid clay, and it gives a firm interior so that these beads can be impressed with stamps.

1 Tear out a 6 in (150mm) square of foil—this will make approximately a 1 in (25mm) bead. Crumple the foil up into a ball in your hands and roll it as you would a ball of clay to compact and round it.

2 Roll out a sheet of clay about ⅛ in (3mm) thick and cut a rough square about 3 in (75mm) across. Wrap the foil ball in this, first wrapping the clay around the middle of the bead, and then folding it down over the ends of the bead.

3 Trim away any surplus clay so that you have an even thickness covering the whole bead. Smooth the joins, and roll the bead in your hands again to make it a regular ball. Place the bead on your work surface and pierce down with a darning needle. The needle should go straight through the foil and the clay. Roll the bead on your palm as usual and then enlarge the hole, if you wish, with a larger sized needle.

BUTTONS

Polymer clay buttons are fun and easy to make. You can use many different techniques to create them.

Making buttons with polymer clay is the home dressmaker's or hand knitter's dream come true! You can mix the clay color to match your garment and use any design you wish to complement or contrast.

Be sure to use one of the stronger brands of clay (see page 125), which will withstand laundering in a washing machine cool wash. If you want to use metallic powders, paint, varnish, or other surface decoration, it is wise to hand wash the buttons only.

These instructions are for making round buttons, but you can make them square, triangular, toggle shaped, or any way you fancy! Take care that the results are smooth and will not catch when the button is worn.

YOU WILL NEED

- *Polymer clay*
- *Ceramic tile*
- *Pen or other tool for impressing the center of the buttons*
- *Thick tapestry or wool needle*

Simple Buttons

1 To make round buttons, follow the instructions for disc beads but make them at least ⅛ in (3mm) thick. Remember that the thickness of the button should be relative to its size, so make larger buttons thicker. Once you have made the discs on the tile impress the centers.

2 The handle of a spoon can be used to make a slot as an alternative, or you can use a stamp made from a small charm (see page 89), or a tiny decorative cutter.

3 Hold the needle upright over each button and pierce down to make two, three, or four holes as you wish. After each piercing action, rotate the needle slightly, still holding it vertically, to enlarge the hole. Bake the buttons on the tile—moving them would distort them. Remove from the tile when they are cool.

TIP

You can use proprietary buttons that are sold for covering with fabric and cover them with polymer clay. Use only those made of metal as they will withstand baking.

Molded Buttons

Polymer clay push molds can be used very successfully to make buttons, and you can make a mold of any button to duplicate it. If you have lost a single button, you can make a mold from one of the others to replace it. See page 56 for how to make and use push molds.

Adding shanks

Molded buttons can be pierced in the usual way or you can add a shank. This is best done when the button is still in the mold. Form a log of clay, about ¼ in (6mm) thick. Cut several ¼ in (6mm) lengths and pierce one through the center of its side with a darning needle. With the darning needle still in place, push one cut end of the log firmly onto the back of the button, using the needle to press down as well. This will give a strong join provided that the buttons are not under-baked.

CABOCHONS

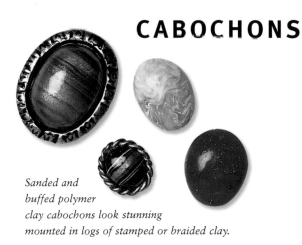

Sanded and buffed polymer clay cabochons look stunning mounted in logs of stamped or braided clay.

The definition of a cabochon is "a gem, polished but not faceted". Cabochons usually have a domed shape with a flat back and are round or oval in shape, although other shapes such as pyramids are found. They are widely used in jewelry, for pendants, rings, or set into brooches and small boxes.

Cabochons are very easy to make in polymer clay and three methods are given here. Use any color of clay for cabochons: marbled mixtures, faux stone mixtures, bone, wood, or inventions of your own. A basic cabochon can also be turned into a cameo—see page 21.

You Will Need

- Polymer clay
- Ceramic tile
- Knife

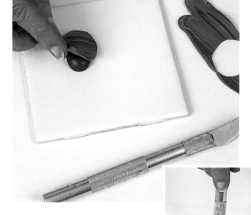

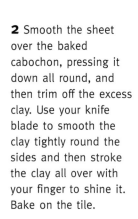

Simple oval cabochon

Form a ½ in (13mm) ball of clay and lightly roll it back and forth in your hands (rather than circling) to shape it into an oval. Place it on a tile and press it down with the flat pad of your finger to shape the upper side into a dome. When it is an even shape, stroke the clay to remove any fingerprints and give it a shine. Bake the cabochon on the tile.

Covered cabochon

1 When you want to make a cabochon using a sheet of clay, perhaps made from slices of millefiori cane or faux onyx, first make and bake a simple cabochon of scrap clay. Cut an oval of clay from your sheet, large enough to cover the cabochon and place it over the cabochon.

2 Smooth the sheet over the baked cabochon, pressing it down all round, and then trim off the excess clay. Use your knife blade to smooth the clay tightly round the sides and then stroke the clay all over with your finger to shine it. Bake on the tile.

Molded cabochon

It is very easy to make a push mold for cabochons and you can use a real cabochon as the master. (See page 56 for instructions on making and using push molds.) To make a cabochon in a push mold, form the clay into a smooth oval and push the best side into the mold, as this will become the top of the cabochon. See page 117 for details of using cabochons and making settings for them.

Millefiori Techniques

This is an almost magical technique that initiated a huge boom in the use of polymer clays during the 1980s and '90s. Polymer clay can be used to create 'canes' of millefiori (which literally means one thousand flowers) in a way that simulates the age-old glass making technique from which it takes its name.

While lacking the transparency of glass, polymer clay has the same ability to be built into a cane, with a pattern running

A cane sheet of simple pinwheel slices, alternated with flower cane slices.

A SIMPLE CUTTER CANE

This is a very easy way of making a simple cane, and you can use any shape of cutter you like. If you have never caned before, follow these instructions first.

YOU WILL NEED

- *Polymer clay: yellow and blue*
- *Cookie cutter; a star, or other simple shape*
- *Knife or sharp blade*

REDUCING CANES

The simplest way to reduce a round log cane is to roll it on your work surface, although this can produce distortion. A good way to reduce canes of all types is to 'pull' the cane.

1 Form a disk of yellow clay, about ³⁄₈ in (10mm) thick, and another of blue. Use the cutter to cut out the star shape from each disc. Insert the blue star into the hole in the yellow disc. You may find it easier to cut out two ¼ in (6mm) stars and press them, one above the other, into the yellow disc.

2 Squeeze the yellow disc all round to make it taller and thinner, keeping the ends as even as possible. When it is about 1 in (25mm) tall, lay it on its side on your work surface and roll it gently to elongate it, just as though it is a log. Keep it even in thickness and press the ends inwards now and then to stop them becoming too distorted.

3 When the cane is about ½ in (13mm) thick, cut it in half to see what the pattern looks like. It should be a perfect, smaller star. If the cane has become too warm from the heat of your hands, you will find it hard to cut neatly, so place it in the refrigerator for 10 minutes.

Lay the cane on your work surface and elongate it by squeezing it along its length and tugging the ends apart. Hold the cane in the air and stroke it downwards, squeezing gently. Periodically, you will need to replace it on your work surface to even it up as the ends will stay larger.

through the center. When the cane is sliced, each slice bears the same image. If the cane is then reduced in diameter, the design becomes smaller. Slices have a multitude of uses including jewelry, or to cover vessels, frames, boxes, and sculptures.

When choosing colors for millefiori, be aware of the need to have strong contrasts in color value. 'Value' is the lightness or darkness of a particular color, and if the values used in canes are too similar, the definition will be poor after the cane is reduced. For this reason, black and white are useful for defining and bordering more subtle colors.

All the canes in this section are about 1 in (25mm) across and 3 in (75mm) long. I find this is the best size to work initially, because it is quicker to handle small quantities of clay and less is wasted if the cane does not work out. When you have made a successful test cane, you can then enlarge all the measurements to make a larger one.

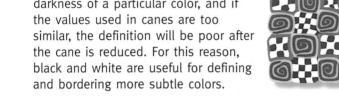

Flower canes give a pretty effect (above), while checkered and spiral canes can make strong images (left).

SLICING CANES

When your cane is reduced to the size you want, it is time to slice it. Lay it on your work surface and cut off the distorted ends. Looking down onto the cane, hold your blade as vertically as you can and cut down firmly in one cut. Roll the cane 90° and cut again. The thickness of your slices will depend on the project, but about $\frac{1}{16}$ in (2mm) is a good guide. Between each cut, try not to move your cutting hand but move the cane towards it. Rolling the cane minimises distortion.

APPLYING CANES TO BEADS

Cane slices are easily applied to beads and can then be rolled in so that no joins are visible. You will need to adjust the size of the slices to the size of beads you want to make.

YOU WILL NEED

- *Polymer clay: cane and matching or contrasting colored clay*
- *Sharp blade*
- *Darning needle*

1 Cut six slices from the cane. Form a round ball for the bead and apply canes evenly all round. You can fill in spaces with slices of a smaller cane.

2 Roll the bead in your hands gently and the slices will sink into the surrounding clay. Keep rolling and you will be able to remove the joins completely.

MAKING CANED SHEETS

These are useful when you want to cover large areas, and to make patterned 'fabric' for sculptures. You can use one design, two or more, or intersperse each patterned cane with a slice of plain log.

YOU WILL NEED

- *Polymer clay canes*
- *Sharp blade*
- *Baking parchment*
- *Roller*

Cut cane slices of equal thickness. Lay them evenly onto the baking parchment so they form a mat. Roll over the surface firmly enough for them to merge together. The baking parchment makes the sheet easy to remove.

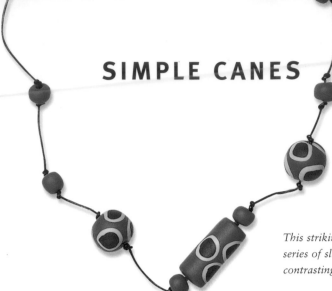

SIMPLE CANES

These are the building blocks of millefiori. Simple canes are, by their nature, quick and easy to do and can be used on their own or combined to make a wonderful variety of complex canes. I find it easiest to divide simple canes by their section shape, and here we cover round, square, and polygonal canes, the last based on a simple triangle.

This striking necklace has been created using a series of slices from a round, bull's-eye cane in contrasting colors.

MANIPULATING THE CLAY

36

YOU WILL NEED

- *Polymer clay in various contrasting colors*
- *Roller or pasta machine*
- *Sharp blade*

ROUND CANES

These are the simplest canes and are used over again in complex cane construction.

Spiral cane

1 Roll out two sheets of clay in contrasting colors, each about ⅛ in (3mm) thick. Place one on top of the other and trim to a rectangular shape about 2½ in (60mm) wide and 5 in (125mm) long. Here, a blended sheet is used as the top sheet over a plain blue sheet. Press down all along one end to thin it.

2 Beginning at the thin end, start rolling the sheets up, making the first turn as tight as possible to avoid any gaps, and continuing rolling tightly to the end. Smooth the end over so that the inner color is covered completely with the outside color. Roll on your work surface to consolidate the cane.

VARIATIONS

- *Use different thicknesses of clay for each sheet*
- *Use two different blends*
- *Make a spiral using a clay wedge and a sheet*

Bull's-eye cane

1 Form a log of clay about ½ in (13mm) thick and trim the ends so it is 3 in (75mm) long. Roll out a sheet of clay, ⅛ in (3mm) thick, cut a strip 3 in (75mm) wide and trim one end. Lay the log across the trimmed end and roll it up in the sheet until the trimmed end touches the sheet. Unroll a little and cut across where the trimmed end will have left a mark.

2 The edges should butt together neatly. Smooth the join and roll a little on your work surface to compress the sheet around the log.

VARIATIONS

- *Wrap a second sheet of color around the cane, or several*
- *Use a striped sheet to wrap the cane*
- *Use a blended log, as in the example left, or wrap a spiral cane*

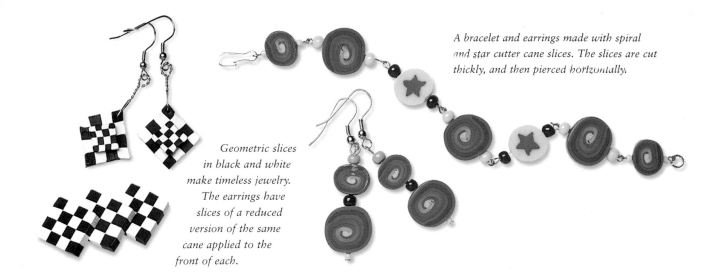

Geometric slices in black and white make timeless jewelry. The earrings have slices of a reduced version of the same cane applied to the front of each.

A bracelet and earrings made with spiral and star cutter cane slices. The slices are cut thickly, and then pierced horizontally.

SQUARE CANES

Square canes are easier to reduce with minimum distortion. Try to make them as accurately as possible—it is more accurate to build them up by stacking sheets than to try to form a square section log. A square or rectangular section cane is sometimes called a 'loaf'.

Striped cane

Roll out two contrasting colored sheets of clay, ⅛ in (3mm) thick and cut them into strips 1 in (25mm) wide and 2½ in (60mm) long. Stack them one on top of the other, alternating the colors. If you are using a pasta machine that will not roll out thick sheets, simply stack two sheets of one color together for each layer.

Check cane

Start with a four-layer striped cane, and use a blade to cut it into four sections longitudinally. Invert every other piece and reassemble into a check cane.

VARIATIONS

- *Use blends for two of the layers*
- *Make six or eight layer checks*
- *Cut the basic cane at an angle and alternate the layers to make chevrons and zigzags*

PINWHEEL

This square cane has its origins in quilting shapes and is very attractive when combined with other square canes, or different versions of itself.

1 Form a square block of clay, with one half blue and the other half orange. It should be approximately a 1 in (25mm) cube. Looking down on the block, use your blade to cut the block accurately into four quarters and then cut across the corners in both directions.

VARIATIONS

- *Use other quilting ideas to make simple blocks like this one to assemble into complex canes*

2 Swap over the resulting triangles to alternate the colors. You will need to upend every other section so that it fits. Reduce the cane by first squeezing it to lengthen it, and then proceeding as usual for a square section cane.

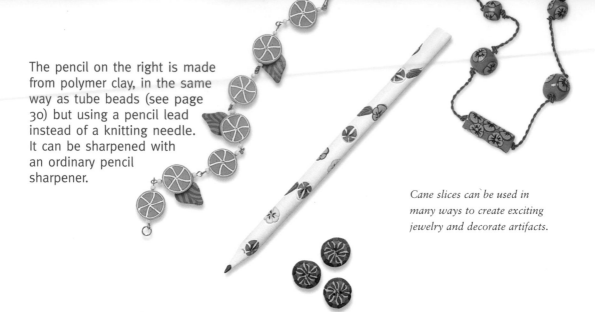

The pencil on the right is made from polymer clay, in the same way as tube beads (see page 30) but using a pencil lead instead of a knitting needle. It can be sharpened with an ordinary pencil sharpener.

Cane slices can be used in many ways to create exciting jewelry and decorate artifacts.

POLYGONAL CANES

These canes are built with triangular canes to give hexagons, or even octagons. They form beautiful canes that can vary from realistic flowers through to fantasy kaleidoscopes, starbursts, spider's webs, and snowflakes.

Orange slice cane

Mix a little orange into translucent clay to make a translucent orange. Wrap with a thin sheet of white. Lay on your work surface and pinch along the top to make the log triangular in shape. Reduce by pulling the cane until it is about $^3/_8$ in (10mm) across. Cut the lengthened cane into six equal parts and assemble with the points together to make a hexagon. Finally, wrap with orange clay and reduce as required.

Flower cane

Wrap a graded blue and white block with black clay. Shape into a triangular cross section, with the white side in the upper point. Reduce the cane and cut into six equal lengths as above. Assemble with the white points together around a thin log of yellow clay.

Kaleidoscope canes

1 These use the same principle as the last two canes but this time, the assembly of the basic triangular cane is purely random. Make several logs of different color clays, compress one or two into flat strips, and include logs of different thicknesses. Press these together in a random way but ensure that the same elements continue along the length of the cane.

2 Reduce the cane, pinch it into a triangular cross section, and cut into six equal lengths. Assemble with the points together, reversing alternate sections so that you have paired patterns. Consolidate it by rolling on the work surface, and then reduce.

VARIATIONS

- *Stack six bull's-eye canes into a triangular cane and use to make a polygonal cane. This will give spider's web effects*
- *Try using various blends for the kaleidoscope canes*

COMPLEX CANES

The name 'complex canes' means that these are formed from several simple canes, not that they are hard to do! Once you have mastered simple canes, it is only a small step to assemble them into intricate patterns. You can alter the section of simple canes by pinching them into a different shape. For example, any round cane can be turned into a square or triangular cane by simply pinching it along its length before reduction.

The beads in this necklace are made using the spiral maze design shown below. Subtle colors such as these give highly sophisticated results.

GEOMETRIC CANES

These are always fun to do and you can get a lot of ideas from patchwork and quilting techniques. Choose colors with plenty of contrast so that the patterns will still be clear after the cane has been reduced.

YOU WILL NEED

- Polymer clay in various contrasting colors
- Roller or pasta machine
- Sharp blade

Spiral maze

1 Make a simple spiral cane and reduce one half to ½ in (13mm) thick and the other half to ⅜ in (10mm) thick. Stand the thicker half upright on your work surface and cut down the center with a blade. Now cut down again to make four quarters.

2 Press the quarters of the larger cane along the outside of the smaller one, placing the points (that were in the center) to the outside. This makes the cane into a square section cane. Reduce until it is ½ in (13mm) across and cut into four equal lengths. Stack the lengths two on two, as shown. The outer spirals will reform to make whole spirals again in a repeat pattern, as the completed green and white cane shows.

Quilt pattern

1 You can stack different simple canes into a repeating quilt pattern to produce delightful effects. Here, a round spiral cane is stacked with a wrapped and an unwrapped check cane to make a four cane block. The spiral canes will be forced into square sections and will distort to fit.

2 On the left, the four canes have been reduced and then stacked again to make a highly detailed result. The cane on the right uses the same technique but the canes were first wrapped in blue, and they show how just a small alteration can give a very different effect.

It is important to remember that this process will distort any internal image and this method is usually used only with plain canes or when a deliberate distortion is required. To change the shape more accurately, you can add extra clay to pack the spaces between assembled canes. You can turn a round cane into a square cane by adding triangular canes at the corners, or you can make a pointed petal flower by adding wedges of clay between the round petals of a simple flower cane.

Face canes combine beautifully with floral canes. Here, a blown hen's egg is covered with cane slices, then baked and sanded smooth.

MANIPULATING THE CLAY

FACE CANES

The Romans and Egyptians made glass face canes over 2000 years ago, so this technique has a noble tradition. You will need to adjust the clay mixtures depending on your brand of clay. All logs should be about 3 in (75mm) long.

COLOR MIXTURES

- *Cheek color = flesh clay + trace of crimson*
- *Lips = flesh clay + slightly more crimson*
- *Face highlights = 8 parts flesh clay + 1 part white*

YOU WILL NEED

- *Polymer clay: flesh, crimson, white, black, blue, brown*
- *Pencil and paper*
- *Roller or pasta machine*
- *Knife*

1 For the eyes, form a ⅛ in (3mm) log of black clay and press on a thin white log. Wrap in a ¹⁄₁₆ in (2mm) blue sheet. Reduce to ³⁄₁₆ in (5mm) thick. Press a triangular cane on each side and wrap in a ¹⁄₃₂ in (1mm) thick brown sheet. Cut in half.

2 Lay a crescent shape of highlight color over each eye, and a larger crescent of shadow on top of that. This should be thicker on the side that lies towards the center of the face. Lay a ¹⁄₃₂ in (1mm) thick sheet of brown over the top of each to make the eyebrow.

3 Press together a log of flesh and a log of highlight color, and form them into a triangle of clay, about ½ in (13mm) long and ⅛ in (3mm) wide at the bottom for the nose. Press the two eyes on either side of this and press a ¹⁄₁₆ in (2mm) thick log of flesh above it between the eyebrows. Make a graded log of cheek color and flesh, with the cheek color in the center. Reduce to ¼ in (6mm) thick, cut in half, and press one under each eye.

4 Form two thin logs of lip color, with a thinner log of flesh centered over them. Press this onto a crimson strip and then press all onto a slightly larger log of lip color with a thinner flesh log on either side. Wrap the whole mouth assembly in thin sheets of flesh, reduce and press onto the bottom of the face. Add packing of flesh as necessary to create a good shape and reduce the cane. The hair is simply spiral canes of brown and black pressed round the face.

- *You can alter the face's appearance by squeezing it in different directions to make it thinner or fatter*

Simple geometric canes in opulent metallic colors surround a face cane for a medieval-style pendant.

Slices of landscape cane are surrounded by logs of black clay that are stamped and silvered to create mounts. The pieces are baked and then linked with wire.

LANDSCAPE CANES

Simple landscapes are not difficult to make, especially if you use blends to suggest distance.

COLOR MIXTURES

- *Mountain violet = 4 parts white + 1 part violet*
- *Pale leaf green = 2 parts white + 1 part leaf green*
- *Olive green = 2 parts leaf green + 1 part light brown*

YOU WILL NEED

- Polymer clay: blue, white, ultramarine blue, violet, turquoise, leaf green, light brown
- Roller or pasta machine
- Knife with pointed blade

1 Make a graded rectangular log for the sky, graded from blue to white, about 1 in (25mm) wide, ½ in (13mm) high, and 3 in (75mm) long. Apply a ⅛ in (3mm) sheet of ultramarine blue to the bottom. Cut out two triangular wedges for the mountains.

2 Form two ¼ in (6mm) logs of mountain violet mix, both 3 in (75mm) long, and pinch them into triangular cross sections. Insert these into the cut out spaces. Trim any surplus off flush with the bottom of the cane.

3 Make a graded rectangular log for the sea, graded from turquoise at the bottom to ultramarine blue at the top. Shape it to the same size as the sky and mountain log and press onto the bottom. Cut away a diagonal section at the bottom right of the cane to make the foreground. Marble lightly together leaf green clay with the two mixed greens, shape into a wedge and press onto the right bottom, trimming any surplus. Reduce the cane as required.

VARIATIONS

- *From this simple basic design, you will find you can make many different canes by varying the mountains, adding different foregrounds, and altering the colors*
- *Try making canes that are just intersecting mountains and sky, with a green foreground, or replacing the sea with graded green or brown wedges for hills*

See also
•
MILLEFIORI TECHNIQUES
PAGE 34-41
BEADS AND BUTTONS
PAGES 28-32

Millefiori with beads and buttons

Combining millefiori with beads and buttons is a perfect marriage of techniques. Millefiori looks particularly beautiful when its intricate designs are applied to jewelry, and its very nature means that patterns can be repeated many times.

This collection combines violet with lime green and silver to make a striking pendant with matching drop earrings. There are also instructions for using the same cane to make buttons, which would look perfect on a violet or black hand knit.

If you wish, you can alter the colors to create a color scheme of your own.

YOU WILL NEED

- *Polymer clay: silver, violet, white, green, yellow*
- *Roller or pasta machine*
- *Sharp blade*
- *Knife*
- *Darning needle*
- *Small square piece of card*
- *Ceramic tile*
- *Small blunt tool for impressing buttons*
- *Fine-nosed jewelry pliers*
- *Two silver-plated head pins*
- *Two silver-plated fish hook earwires*
- *Six silver lined ⅛ in (3mm) glass beads*

DROP EARRINGS

1 Make a flower cane (see page 38), using graded violet and white clay logs wrapped in silver and assembled round a yellow log. Make a round cane with a yellow center grading to green, wrap with silver and pinch into a triangular cross-section. Press four 2 in (50mm) lengths of this onto a 2 in (50mm) length of the round cane to suggest leaves. Reduce the square cane to ½ in (13mm) across.

2 To make the beads, form two ³/₄ in (19mm) balls of silver clay. Press four slices of the cane around the center of each, placing them at a 45° angle. The points should just touch. Do not roll them into the bead but leave proud for an embossed effect. Make two more plain silver beads, ¹/₂ in (13mm) in diameter.

3 Pierce all four beads in the usual way. Roll the decorated beads very lightly on your hand after piercing so that the cane slices are not flattened. Bake for 20 minutes.

4 To assemble each earring, thread a glass bead onto a head pin, then a large millefiori bead, another glass bead, the small plain silver bead, and finally another glass bead. Trim the head pin to ¹/₄ in (6mm) from the top bead and turn a small loop. Attach to one of the earwires.

PENDANT

1 Roll out a sheet of silver clay, ¹/₈ in (3mm) thick. Lay a square piece of card on the sheet for a guide and cut a right angle for the bottom of the pendant.

2 Use the piece of card as a guide to cut the two side corners of the pendant and leave a ¹/₄ in (6mm) wide strip extending from the top corner, as shown. The pendant sides should be 1 in (25mm) long and the strip should extend ¹/₂ in (13mm). Turn the pendant over and mark decorative lines on the strip with the side of a needle.

3 Turn the pendant over again and curl the strip up around the needle to make a loop, pressing it down onto itself to secure. Cut four cane slices and press onto the front of the pendant. After baking, the pendant can be threaded onto a silver chain or a thong.

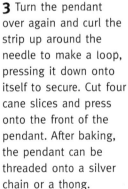

BUTTONS

1 Flatten a ¹/₂ in (13mm) ball of silver clay onto the tile, following the button making instructions on page 32. Reduce a length of the flower cane to ¹/₄ in (6mm) diameter, and press two slices opposite each other on the button. Reduce the green cane to ³/₁₆ in (5mm) across and flatten into an oval cross-section. Cut slices to represent leaves and press onto either side of the flowers.

2 Impress the center of each button with a round tool and then make two holes. Bake the buttons on the tile for 20 minutes, or according to the manufacturers' instructions.

MOSAICS

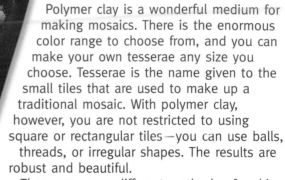

The pietre dure panel, dolphin micro-mosaic brooch, and floral appliqué pendant are all made with polymer clay mosaic techniques.

Polymer clay is a wonderful medium for making mosaics. There is the enormous color range to choose from, and you can make your own tesserae any size you choose. Tesserae is the name given to the small tiles that are used to make up a traditional mosaic. With polymer clay, however, you are not restricted to using square or rectangular tiles—you can use balls, threads, or irregular shapes. The results are robust and beautiful.

There are many different methods of making polymer clay mosaics and three of them are given here: pre-baked tesserae mosaic; soft-on-soft micro mosaic; and pietre dure mosaic.

MANIPULATING THE CLAY

FLOWERPOT MOSAIC

The following project uses a small terracotta flowerpot as a base. You may need to adjust the design depending on the size of the flowerpot you use. You could also cover tablemats, table tops, lamp bases, flowerpots, plates, wall panels—the list of possibilities is endless.

VARIATION

- *Mosaics can be made in a wonderful array of color schemes and designs. If you want to make more elaborate patterns, try cutting your tesserae smaller for detailed areas and using larger sizes for the background*

YOU WILL NEED

- *Polymer clay: translucent, white, pink, leaf green, dark grey, burgundy. You will need about ½ oz (15g) of clay in each color*
- *Knife*
- *Baking sheet lined with paper or baking parchment*
- *3½ in (90mm) diameter terracotta flowerpot*
- *PVA glue*
- *Matt varnish and brush*
- *Spackle (interior wall filler)*
- *Small bowl, sponge, and rag*

1 First cut up the clay. Cut a block into bars about ¼ in (6mm) square, and an inch or two long. Now cut 1⁄16 in (2mm) thick slices from the bar, keeping the slices as close to the same size and thickness as you can.

2 Pile the tesserae onto the baking sheet, spreading them out lightly. There is no need to keep them separate—although they will stick together slightly when baked, you will be able to separate them after baking.

PRE-BAKED TESSERAE MOSAIC

This method of making mosaics with polymer clay is probably the easiest, and is great fun to do. Blocks of clay are sliced up into small tesserae about ¼ in (6mm) square. They are then baked and glued onto various surfaces to create the mosaic. The best type of clay to use for pre-baked tesserae is one of the firmer brands. This is often a useful way to use up old blocks of clay that have gone too hard. There is no need to knead the clay first and it is easier to cut squares straight from the block. You can also make mixtures of clay from the recipes for simulated semi-precious stones, but leave the mix to cool in the refrigerator for 30 minutes before cutting.

Pre-baked tesserae glued to a ceramic tile makes a delightful table mat.

3 When the tesserae have cooled, apply glue to one side of the flowerpot top. Press a line of transparent tesserae onto the glue, following the line of the top of the pot and butting the tesserae together. If the occasional tessera is too large, trim it to size with your knife. When the first row is complete, make another, butting up to the first. Work on one section of the flowerpot at a time.

4 If your flowerpot has a ridge, first glue a line of dark gray tesserae just under it, then glue a line on the ridge itself, angled slightly so that it covers the ridge and butts against the upper row. You may need to trim the tesserae to make them fit.

5 Work down the flowerpot, adding another row of transparent tesserae, then making a rectangle of leaf green and pink. Add another row of transparent, and then a final row of dark gray, adjusting the design to fit the size of your flowerpot. Let the glue dry for a while and then complete the rest of the flowerpot to match. Leave to dry overnight.

6 Varnish the mosaic liberally with matt varnish. This will seal the surface of the tesserae and prevent the grout from spoiling them. It will also help to consolidate the tesserae onto the flowerpot. Allow the varnish to dry.

7 Mix up some wall filler to the consistency of thin cream. Use a sponge to apply it to the mosaic, pushing it down into the gaps between the tesserae. Use a damp rag to wipe away the excess while it is still wet. When the grout is dry, you can use a stiff brush and water to scrub away any grout that is left over the surface of the tesserae. You will find they are surprisingly robust!

SOFT-ON-SOFT MOSAIC

This technique is useful for creating micro-mosaics for jewelry, and uses a knife with a curved blade to apply tiny, soft tesserae to a soft background of clay.

I developed this method when I became frustrated at how long it took to make micro mosaics with baked tesserae!

The soft colors of this brooch simulate the muted effects of Roman mosaics. You can find further inspiration from the wonderful mosaics of other ancient cultures, and many are reproduced in books or can be seen in museums.

ROMAN PANEL

The design demonstrated here is inspired by Roman mosaics, which often contained animal and bird motifs.

YOU WILL NEED

- *Tracing paper and pencil*
- *Polymer clay: beige, dark brown, black, dark green, copper, violet, light green, pale blue, light pink, dark pink, gold or light brown*
- *Darning needle*
- *Knife with a curved blade*
- *Ceramic tile*

USING MICRO-MOSAICS

This little panel makes a beautiful brooch but there are many other ways to use micro-mosaics.

- *On box lids*
- *Set into cup findings for pendants, brooches, and earrings*
- *Applied to beads and buttons*

When a micro-mosaic is to be worn, give it a coat of matt varnish to ensure that none of the squares are damaged with wear.

1 Trace the template onto the tracing paper. Roll out some beige clay, ⅛ in (3mm) thick, on the tile. Lay the template on the clay and cut out the shape, removing the waste clay. Draw over the lines on the paper with the darning needle to make an impression on the clay and give guide lines for the mosaic.

2 Roll out dark brown clay, ⅟₁₆ in (2mm) thick and cut a bar of clay, ⅟₁₆ in (2mm) wide. Position this near the tile, at a comfortable angle, and cut a slice with your knife, using the very tip of the blade. Scoop up the slice, which will have a square cross section just like a tiny tesserae. It should stick to your blade with the clay's natural tackiness.

TEMPLATE
Use a photocopier to enlarge or reduce the template if you wish.

The shape of the knife blade is important because it allows you to cut each tessera, scoop it onto the blade, and then apply it to the clay base in one rapid movement. It is very difficult to apply such tiny pieces of soft clay to a mosaic with your fingers.

The bee brooch uses translucent clay mixed with blue for the wings, which adds depth to the design.

This geometric design is based on Islamic tile patterns. Strong, contrasting colors give impact to geometric pieces.

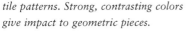

3 Turn the knife blade over so that the little square is underneath and press it down onto the line marking the duck's back. You should angle it so that it is positioned along the line. When the square touches the soft clay base, it should stick there and you can remove the knife. Cut another slice and repeat, placing a row of squares along the duck's back.

4 Continue applying dark brown squares to outline the duck, always angling them in the direction of the line they are on. Cut a bar of black clay in the same way, but make it slightly thinner, and use squares of this to outline the duck's beak. Apply a square of black for the duck's eye.

5 Cut bars of dark green, violet, and beige. Using the photographs as a guide, fill in the areas of color within the outline, angling the squares round the head, across the neck, and down the breast.

6 Use copper for the duck's back and tail; light blue, dark brown, and beige for the water; and dark and light green for the leaves. The lilies are light and dark pink, while the beak is gold. Once the duck and foreground are completed, cut a larger bar of beige clay and cut and apply squares all round the outside of the piece.

7 Fill in the rest of the background in regular parallel lines. You will need to cut parts of squares to fit neatly into any spaces between the duck and the lines of background. Press over the mosaic lightly with your finger to consolidate the squares and ensure they are pressed firmly down. Bake the mosaic on the tile for at least 20 minutes.

APPLIQUÉ

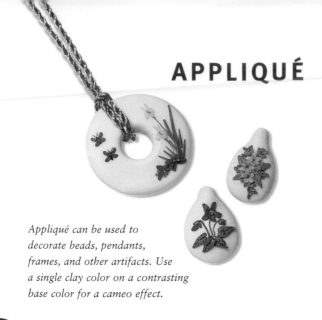

Appliqué can be used to decorate beads, pendants, frames, and other artifacts. Use a single clay color on a contrasting base color for a cameo effect.

Although this technique is not actually a mosaic, it is included here because it uses a variation on the soft-on-soft method of applying clay. Logs of various cross sections are sliced with the knife to produce slices of many different shapes. These are then applied to a base layer of clay to give exquisite cameo effects. You can use slices cut from a clay extruder, or shape the logs yourself, or even use clay shapes cut with tiny cutters.

Because the base layer remains visible, you need to choose a color that will tone or contrast with the appliqué. Marble, pearl, or simulated stone clays all look particularly attractive for this.

FLOWER PENDANT

The leaves in the following sequence are modeled and not sliced to give a more convincing leaf shape.

YOU WILL NEED

- *Polymer clay: pearl, leaf green, pink, pale blue, black*
- *Knife with a curved blade*
- *Blunt tapestry needle*

VARIATIONS

This technique can be used in many ways to create beautiful jewelry. Try adding butterflies and birds to your appliqué or creating recognizable flowers, such as lilies and roses.

1 Make a cabochon using the pearl clay (see page 33), about 1⅛ in (28mm) by ¾ in (19mm). Smooth over the surface with the pad of your finger to remove fingerprints. Form a ⅛ in (3mm) log of leaf green and cut several ⅛ in (3mm) lengths. Form each of these into a teardrop and press down on the work surface to flatten it into a leaf shape. Press lightly onto the cabochon. Mark veins with your knife.

2 Form a ⅛ in (3mm) log of pink clay for the petals and flatten it slightly to give an oval cross section. Cut a slice with the tip of your knife, lift it on your knife, and then press it down onto the leaves. You should position the point of your knife where you want the center of the flower to go. Cut another slice and apply, overlapping the center of the first petal. Continue round the flower, applying five or six petals evenly. Always work round the flower in one direction so that the flat side of each petal lies in the same direction.

3 Form a 1/16 in (2mm) log of pale blue clay and cut slices for the tiny flowers. Apply these in sprays around the leaves and larger flower. Apply a similar sized slice of black to the center of the large flower. Use the needle to make holes in the center of these smaller slices. When the appliqué is finished, pat all over it lightly with your finger to consolidate the applied pieces before baking.

PIETRE DURE

Pietre dure is a glorious type of mosaic that was developed in 16th Century Florence. It is possible to simulate this ancient technique with polymer clay to create beautiful pieces for jewelry or boxes.

This technique was inspired by a trip to Florence where I saw my first real pietre dure mosaics. Pietre dure means "hard stones" in Italian, and semi-precious stones are the

The volcano Mount St. Helens, Washington, was the inspiration for this scenic pietre dure panel.

STILL LIFE PANEL

This project uses a typical motif of pears on a branch with a black background. It is very important to roll out the clay to the same thickness throughout this project so that the added pieces will fit precisely into the background clay.

YOU WILL NEED

- *Polymer clay: black, dark brown, gold, dark leaf green, light leaf green, violet, white, golden yellow, copper*
- *Two ceramic tiles*
- *Roller and card strips, or pasta machine*
- *2½ in (60mm) round cutter, or piece of card cut out in a circle of this size*

- *Tracing paper and pencil*
- *Darning needle*
- *Knife with a long, thin, pointed blade*
- *Talcum powder*
- *Blunt tapestry needle*
- *Sand paper: 600 and 800 grit*
- *Quilt wadding or denim fabric for buffing*

The finished piece after baking, sanding, and buffing.

1 Roll out some black clay on the tile, ¹⁄₁₆ in (1.5mm) thick. Cut out a round shape with the cutter, or cut round a circle of card with your knife. Trace the template and lay it on the clay. Draw firmly over the lines with the darning needle to mark the design onto the clay below.

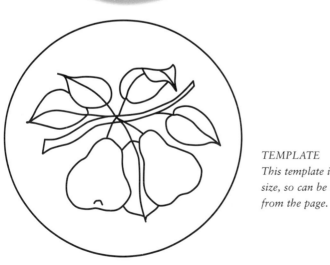

TEMPLATE
This template is shown actual size, so can be traced directly from the page.

material used to create these spectacular art forms. The technique is used to create tabletops, wall panels, tomb decorations, jewelry, and many other artifacts. The subject matter varies from Florentine scenes to birds, flowers, and many types of still life. While most mosaics are made up of small tesserae, pietre dure uses larger sections cut from a sheet of variable colored semi-precious stone, which are fitted together rather like marquetry.

Marbled sheets of clay are used for spectacular sky effects in landscape pietre dure.

MANIPULATING THE CLAY

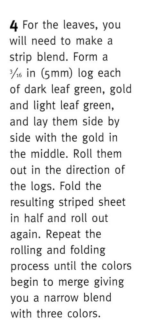

2 Marble together some gold and brown clay and roll it out to the same thickness as the background. Holding the knife as vertically as possible, cut out the shape of the branch from the background. Remove it carefully with the tip of your knife, taking care not to damage the background—it does not matter if the piece you are removing is not a perfect shape.

3 Smear a little talcum powder over the marbled clay and lay the removed piece on top; this is your template for the branch. Cut round this shape as accurately as you can. Remove the black clay template, carefully lift out the cut out branch, and press it into the hole in the background.

4 For the leaves, you will need to make a strip blend. Form a ³⁄₁₆ in (5mm) log each of dark leaf green, gold and light leaf green, and lay them side by side with the gold in the middle. Roll them out in the direction of the logs. Fold the resulting striped sheet in half and roll out again. Repeat the rolling and folding process until the colors begin to merge giving you a narrow blend with three colors.

5 Cut out half of one of the leaves from the background, cutting out the edge and then down the middle. Powder the leaf blend, and lay the cut out piece diagonally across the stripes. Cut out the half leaf and lift it into the space. Repeat for the second half of the leaf, but this time with the leaf point facing in the other direction so that the colors will be staggered when placed together.

I have found that the most successful method of simulating pietre dure in polymer clay is to work with soft clay. A background sheet of clay is traced with the design and sections are cut from this. The resulting spaces are filled with different colored clays, some marbled, some as narrow blends. The finished result is remarkably like real pietre dure and it is an exciting technique to use.

Birds are a traditional pietre dure motif. Multi-colored strip blends can be used for brilliant feathers.

6 The other leaves are made in the same way. The pears are made using a strip blend of golden yellow grading to copper. Each pear should be cut out with the shaded copper part towards the bottom right to indicate an area of shadow.

7 To create the highlight on the pear, make a hole with the tapestry needle and fill with a small ball of white clay, smoothing it in. To make the pear stems, mark a groove with the tapestry needle. Roll a very thin log of the marbled brown and gold clay and press this into the groove. Complete the other pear and remaining leaves and stems in the same way.

8 When the piece is finished, place a fresh piece of tracing paper on top and burnish over the surface with the pad of your finger to smooth out any bumps and holes. Finally, lay the tracing paper on top and cover with another tile. Bake for at least 40 minutes (see page 20 for instructions on baking sheets). When the pietre dure is cool, keep it on the tile for support and sand and buff to thoroughly smooth the surface.

VARIATIONS

- *The photographs above show other designs of pietre dure that you can try*
- *Pietre dure sheets can be assembled into beautiful boxes (see page 68)*

TEXTILE EFFECTS

There are few modeling materials that have such an outstanding ability to simulate other materials as polymer clay. This section shows you how it can be used to make an extraordinary variety of textile effects.

Miniature polymer clay curtains can be painted with acrylic paint motifs to suggest a patterned fabric.

This doll brooch uses texturing, gathering, lace effects, and a polymer clay bow.

TEXTURING

The best textiles to use for this technique are those with a definite texture, such as plain cottons and, for more fancy effects, braids, brocades, and lace.

YOU WILL NEED

- *Polymer clay*
- *Talcum powder*
- *Roller or pasta machine*
- *Fabric for texturing*

1 Roll out the clay to $\frac{1}{16}$ in (2mm) thick or less. Place the clay on a work surface lightly dusted with talcum powder. Lay the fabric on the clay and roll over it firmly with your roller. Peel off the fabric to leave the impression.

2 If you bake the impressed sheets flat, you can then use them to make a positive impression on another sheet of clay. Here, the sheet impressed with bobbin lace has been used to impress the black clay. You can then pick out the relief of the delicate lace forms by brushing on gold wax paste, metallic powders, or pastels (see pages 90 and 91).

LACE

Lace can be made by using real lace to texture the clay or you can make your own lace by crimping the edge of a thin strip and impressing it with little holes to suggest broderie anglais.

YOU WILL NEED

- *Polymer clay: white*
- *Roller*
- *Talcum powder*
- *Scalloped cookie (pastry) cutter*
- *Large needle*

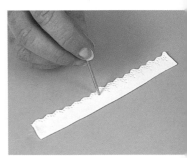

1 Roll out a thin strip of clay, $\frac{1}{16}$ in (2mm) thick, $\frac{3}{8}$ in (10mm) wide and as long as required. Cut along one long side with the cookie cutter to give a scalloped edge. Use talcum powder to prevent sticking.

2 Use the needle to make a line of punctured holes along the scalloped edge of the lace. Then make little clusters of holes at regular intervals to decorate the lace further. It is a good idea to look at different types of lace to give you ideas for making your own. The lace strip can then be either gathered or frilled.

Polymer clay can be rolled into extremely thin sheets and still retain considerable strength and flexibility. It will also take fine and detailed impressions, and these two qualities mean that it can be used to simulate many different textiles. From delicate lace to homespun fabrics, cloth of gold to ribbons and bows—all can be created using polymer clay. Once formed, it can be cut and assembled just like fabric, but without the sewing! It can be gathered and frilled, and you can even simulate stitching, pin tucking, quilting, and patchwork. If you use caned sheets (see page 35), you can have patterned fabric as well.

Textile effects can be used in many different ways. Sculpted figures can be draped or clothed (see page 80), tiny doll brooches can be festooned with lace and ribbons, and fabric miniatures easily formed. Simulated leather is also remarkably realistic in polymer clay.

The different brands of clay vary as to how easy they are to use for fabric effects. Avoid the softer clays and those with a very tacky surface. It is also best to use stronger clays, as simulating textiles inevitably involves using thin sheets. (See page 125 for details of the different brands available.)

GATHERING

It is easy to gather polymer clay 'fabric' and you do not need to sew it!

1 Hold one end of the edge to be gathered in one hand. With the other hand, make a fold in the top edge, about ½ in (13mm) in from the end and squeeze it lightly to secure. Move along about another ½ in (13mm) and make another fold. Repeat all the way along, spacing each fold evenly and pressing to secure.

YOU WILL NEED

● *Thin sheet of polymer clay fabric or lace*

2 Lace strips are gathered in the same way and you can gather them into rosettes or straight sections. You can vary how much you gather a fabric by how large each fold is and how far apart the folds are spaced. You need a light touch for gathering so that the thin clay is not crushed in the heat of your hands.
Once the fabric or lace is gathered, it can simply be pressed onto the sculpture or jewelry as required.

RIBBON BOWS

These are useful in innumerable ways: for jewelry; novelty pins and brooches such as teddy bears and dolls; and for simulating ribbon bows in miniatures.

1 Form a ¹⁄₁₆ in (1.5mm) thick log of clay and roll it flat to make a thin strip, about ¹⁄₃₂ in (1mm) thick and ⅛ in (3mm) wide. Cut two 1 in (25mm) lengths for the ribbon streamers and place them in a 'V' as shown. Trim the bottom edges into points with your knife. Cut another length of strip, 1¾ in (45mm) long and fold in the two ends to make the loops of the bow.

YOU WILL NEED

● *Polymer clay*
● *Roller*
● *Knife*

2 Pinch the center of the bow to make it thinner and slightly gathered. Wrap the center with a small length of the strip. Lift the bow on your knife, and place onto the top of the two streamers. Press down lightly to secure. You can curl, ripple, or drape the ends of the streamers.

BASKET WEAVING

What fun to be able to make baskets of your own, in any size, shape or color, and with polymer clay. This is not a difficult technique and one that children can enjoy.

The completed baskets show the pleasing textures of woven polymer clay. Baskets can be made in a wide variety of designs, and you can find inspiration in the traditional basketry of different cultures.

MINIATURE BASKET

YOU WILL NEED

● *Polymer clay: ocher, dark brown*

1 Roll out a long thin log of ocher clay, about $\frac{1}{16}$ in (2mm) thick and at least 6 in (150mm) long. Try to keep the log an even thickness all along its length. Fold the log in half to double it, and twist the ends in opposite directions to make an even rope.

2 Begin by coiling the basket base. Start with a tiny loop of rope and then coil round and round, twisting the rope with each coil so that it does not unwind.

3 When the base is about $1\frac{1}{4}$ in (30mm) across, begin to coil up the sides of the basket. When each rope runs out, add in another and continue coiling, pinching each coil onto the last lightly to consolidate the basket. Finish the top of the basket with a coil of rope made from an ocher and a brown log twisted together.

4 To make the two lug handles, cut two $\frac{3}{4}$ in (19mm) lengths of the two-color log, shape each into a curve and press inside the top of the basket. Bake for about 15 minutes.

WOVEN BASKET

You can make this basket in riotous color mixtures for some unusual effects. The basket is $2\frac{1}{2}$ in (60mm) across and 2 in (50mm) tall, but the technique can make bigger baskets.

YOU WILL NEED

● *Polymer clay: purple, violet, turquoise green*
● *Roller*
● *Scalloped cookie (pastry) cutter*
● *Thick tapestry needle, about $\frac{1}{8}$ in (3mm) thick*
● *Superglue*
● *Sharp scissors*

VARIATION

● *Make lids for your baskets by simply coiling a disc of clay to the right size and baking it on a tile*

The first technique shown here demonstrates how to simply twist the clay into a rope and coil this to make a miniature basket. While you can do this without any support for baskets under about 2 in (50mm) across, if you want to work larger, use a support such as a jelly (jam) jar or a matchbox upon which to coil the clay. You could even coil clay onto one of your own vessels (see pages 62–67).

The second technique uses a baked base and uprights to provide the support for weaving the soft clay into a basket. This is a good compromise between softness and hardness, although you can weave a basket using baked weavers but they can be quite fragile unless you use a flexible clay (see page 125).

This basket was made by coiling marbled ropes of clay over an upturned cereal bowl, then baking on the bowl.

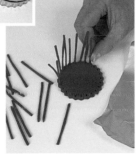

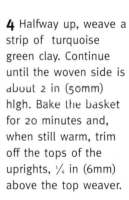

1 Roll out a ⅛ in (3mm) thick sheet of violet clay and cut out a scalloped disc with the cutter. Using the scallops as a guide, pierce a hole in each with a thick tapestry needle all the way round the edge of the disc. Roll out a long log of clay, about ³/₃₂ in (2.5mm) thick and cut as many 2½ in (60mm) lengths as there are holes in the disc. Roll each log on the work surface to point one end slightly.

2 Bake the disk and logs for 20 minutes. When they are cool, pour some superglue onto a piece of foil, dip the pointed tip of a log into the glue, and immediately press it into a hole in the disc, holding it upright to set. Work round the disc, inserting logs. Do not worry if they are not perfectly upright, as they will straighten when you weave.

3 When all the logs are in place, roll out a long log of purple clay, ⅛ in (3mm) thick and begin weaving in and out around the upright logs. Weave two rows, making the second row alternate with the first and pushing any ends through to the inside. Now make a ⅛ in (3mm) log and roll it flat to form a strip ¼ in (6mm) wide. Use this to weave up the basket, alternating each row.

4 Halfway up, weave a strip of turquoise green clay. Continue until the woven side is about 2 in (50mm) high. Bake the basket for 20 minutes and, when still warm, trim off the tops of the uprights, ¼ in (6mm) above the top weaver.

5 Using a ³/₁₆ in (5mm) thick log of violet clay, weave round the top of the uprights, making a loop round each. Press the clay down lightly to consolidate it and bake again for 20 minutes.

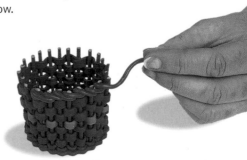

MOLDING

Here is yet another extraordinary quality of polymer clay: not only can you mold it in push molds and two-part molds, you can also make the very molds out of polymer clay. Polymer clay is ideal for molding techniques

This necklace was made using several different types of beads molded in two-part molds. The red beads are glass.

PUSH MOLDS

These are the simplest form of mold but are often the most useful. Pieces made in a push mold can only have the front and sides molded and will usually have a flat back.

MATERIALS

- *Polymer clay: any scrap clay, gold for the molded piece*
- *A form to make a mold from—here an antique carved wooden box top*
- *Talcum powder*
- *Soft brush*

1 Brush the box lid lightly with talcum powder and brush off the excess. Form a well-kneaded ball of clay, big enough to cover the box lid when it is flattened. Flatten it into a disc, slightly larger than the box lid. Smear with talcum powder over one surface.

2 Press the powdered surface of the disc firmly onto the box top, working the clay about ¼ in (6 mm) down the sides and trying not to let it move around or you will get a double impression. When you are sure that it is firmly pressed down all over the box top, gently ease it off. If the mold distorts as you remove it, just gently pull it back into shape. Bake the mold for 30 minutes, so that it is as hard as possible.

3 To make a casting, brush the inside of the mold lightly with talcum powder. Form a disc of gold clay with no folds or creases in the clay surface. It should be slightly thicker than the mold interior, but of a smaller diameter so that it is easy to push in.

4 Press the disk firmly into the mold, pushing it in all round. Be careful that the clay does not shift in the mold once you have pressed it in or you will get a double image. You can trim the back with your knife if necessary.

5 Ease the clay out of the mold by pushing the sides inwards until you can pull it out. If the clay distorts, you can place it on your work surface and push it back into shape. Trim round the outside of the molding with your knife to neaten it. Here the molding in the foreground was made from simulated bone and then 'aged' with acrylics (see page 115).

because of its fine texture and ability to take impressions. Virtually any textured surface or intricate shape can be faithfully reproduced in the clay by simply pressing it against the object to be duplicated. These instructions show you how to make your own molds using the clay and then how to make

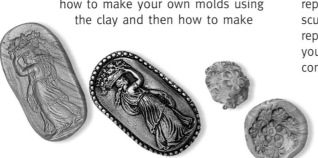

reproductions from those molds.

There are countless applications for these techniques, from duplicating lost buttons to replicating carvings on wood or stone, moldings on plaster or intricate metal engravings. You can reproduce the face of an antique porcelain sculpture to incorporate into jewelry, or reproduce your own sculpted dolls' faces. Once you start making your own molds, you will constantly find more uses for them.

Two molded pieces and their respective push molds. The larger piece is brushed with metallic paste, the smaller with artists' pastels.

TWO-PART MOLDS

These are not difficult to make and are extremely useful for duplicating three-dimensional objects such as carved or engraved beads and miniature sculptures. The bead here is metal so it can remain in the mold during baking. If your original cannot be baked, you will need to remove it first. Two colors are used for the mold so that if the two parts stick together, it will be easy to see where to separate them.

YOU WILL NEED

- *Polymer clay: two colors of scrap for the mold, black for the molded bead*
- *Talcum powder*
- *Bead for a master to make the mold*
- *Thick tapestry needle*

1 Make an ordinary push mold as opposite using the bead. The clay should come exactly half way up the outside of the bead. Poke four registration holes in the push mold. Bake the mold with the bead in place for at least 20 minutes.

2 Dust the bead and the mold top liberally with talcum powder. Press a disc of a second color of clay onto the top of the bead and the lower mold to make the top half of the mold. The soft clay will fill the registration holes to give a key. Bake the mold again with the bead in place. When cold, the two parts should separate easily.

3 To use the mold, dust both parts well with talcum powder, including the flanged surfaces where the molds meet. Form a ball of black clay, the same size as the original bead, and press it into the lower mold. Press on the top mold, aligning the registration holes and posts. Push down hard. Open the mold, ease out the bead, and use your knife to remove any flashing round the bead. Pierce the bead in the usual way.

GOLD CLAY EFFECTS

Some metallic and pearlescent polymer clays, and gold clay in particular, can be manipulated to create effects that are almost holographic in appearance. These clays contain mica, and it is light reflecting off mica particles that gives the stunning results.

Cane slices applied to clay sheets and rolled flat make spectacular veneers.

CANING

When the gold clay is rolled out flat, folded in half, and rolled out again repeatedly, all the mica particles become aligned with their flat surfaces facing up. If these sheets are stacked to make a block, the top and bottom surfaces of the block will shine with gold and all the side surfaces will look dull. You can then create different effects in a cane, depending on which way you turn parts of the block.

YOU WILL NEED

For all gold techniques

- *Polymer clay: gold*
- *Roller or pasta machine*
- *Blade*
- *Knife with a curved blade*
- *Talcum powder*
- *Stamp*

1 Roll out about half a block of the gold clay to make a sheet ⅛ in (3mm) thick. Fold the sheet in half and roll out again. Continue folding and rolling until the surface of the clay becomes a smooth shiny gold. Cut the sheet into 2 in (50mm) squares and stack to make a ½ in (13mm) high block.

2 Cut the block in half and you will find that the cut edges of the sides are dull, while the top and bottom are bright gold. Lay one half on top of the other and cut again. This will give you two 1 in (25mm) blocks.

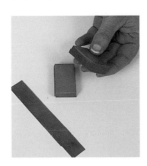

3 Turn one of the blocks on its side and cut a slice from the shiny side. The new surface revealed will be bright gold and this will continue through the block. Similarly, any slice cut from the dull side will always reveal a dull surface. You can now alternate these slices in layers to make a striped cane. Do not try to reduce the cane or the effects will be lost.

4 You can make the striped cane into a check cane in the usual way (see page 36). Slices cut from gold canes can be applied to beads or vessels, or laid on a bright gold sheet and rolled in to make beautiful patterned sheets or veneers.

Mica particles are rather like tiny discs that will shine when their flat surfaces are exposed to light but look dull when viewed end-on. It is this quality that is utilized to create these beautiful reflections. Not all clays reflect in this way, so check the chart on page 125 for the best clays for this technique.

A photograph does not do this technique justice, because it is when you move the piece to catch the light that the highlights change within the clay. Sanding and buffing will bring out the reflections even more.

These techniques were pioneered by Pier Voulkos, Mike Buesseler, and others in the USA.

A pendant with ghost impressions and jewelry made with filigree gold clay.

GOLD APPLIQUÉ TECHNIQUE

This uses the appliqué technique explained on page 48 to make designs in dark gold on a bright gold base. It can be applied to beads or sheets of clay. If you use a sheet, roll the appliqué in lightly with a roller.

Cut a bar from the block so that the end is dark clay. Shape into a log with an oval cross section. Wrap a ball of clay in a sheet of gold so that the ball is covered in bright gold. Apply slices of dark gold to make flower shapes, roll into the bead, and pierce.

FILIGREE EFFECTS

If thin strips of clay are cut from the gold block, the sides will be dark gold and the top and bottom bright gold. These can then be twisted to make lovely two-tone twists to use for filigree and mountings.

Roll out the gold sheet to 1/16 in (2mm) thick. Cut several 1/16 in (2mm) thick strips—a long straight blade makes this much easier. Twist the two ends of a strip in opposite directions to make it evenly twisted all along its length. You can now apply coils to sheets of clay for decorative effects or make spirals for earrings and pins.

GHOST IMPRESSIONS

This is another mystical effect. If the gold block is impressed with a stamp and then pared back to smooth clay, the image is still visible as the mica has been compressed below the surface.

Stack gold sheets to make a block about 1/4 in (6mm) high. Smooth talcum powder over the surface and impress with the stamp. Use your blade to pare back the top layers of clay, taking thin slices, until you are just below the impressed area. The image will still be there and can be rolled lightly.

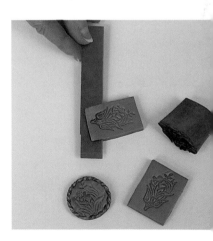

VARIATIONS

- *Spiral canes are made by rolling up a sheet cut from the top of a layered block with a sheet cut from the side*
- *Disc canes are simply a rolled-up sheet of clay that gives a "C.D." effect when sliced*

FLOWER TECHNIQUES

Polymer clay can be used to make pieces of extreme delicacy, and flower techniques demonstrate this more than any other. The clay can be rolled out as thin as $\frac{1}{32}$ in (1mm) for shaping into highly realistic flowers and leaves, while the pastel and translucent colors enhance the delicate beauty of the results.

Dainty primroses bound into a corsage with green florist's tape. They would look equally charming in a hat!

PRIMROSES

These instructions use primrose gum paste cutters but you could cut out the shapes using your knife instead. You can adapt the technique to make many other flowers and there are many books available on gum paste craft (sugarcraft) that will give you further ideas.

YOU WILL NEED

- Polymer clay: yellow, translucent, golden yellow, leaf green
- Baking parchment
- Talcum powder
- Primrose cutter
- Blunt tapestry needle
- Rounded flat modeling tool
- Small calyx cutter
- Fine florist's wire
- Jelly (jam) jar
- Wooden skewer
- Primrose leaf or any leaf with well-defined veins. Alternatively, use a leaf cutter and veiner from cake decorating shops
- Foil

MIXTURES

- *Primrose yellow = 8 parts translucent + 1 part yellow*
- *Pale leaf green = 8 parts translucent + 1 part leaf green*

1 Form a $\frac{1}{2}$ in (13mm) ball of primrose yellow and shape it into a teardrop. Press the wider end of the teardrop down onto the baking parchment and press all round the edge to make a little Mexican hat shape as shown. Keep a small cone of clay sticking up in the center and press out the surrounding clay until it is less than $\frac{1}{16}$ in (2mm) thick and about $1\frac{1}{4}$ in (30mm) across.

2 Dust the clay with talcum powder. Place the cutter's central hole over the cone of clay and press down firmly to cut out the flower.

3 Peel the paper away from the clay and then use the needle to carefully ease the clay out of the cutter. If it distorts, just pinch it back into shape.

4 Dust your fingers with talcum powder to prevent the clay sticking. Hold the flower by its cone and pierce into the center with the needle to make the flower into a little trumpet. Now use the modeling tool to press each petal against your finger to thin and cup it. Make the edges as thin as possible for a truly realistic look.

These techniques borrow from the world of cake decorating, where realistic flowers are made with gum paste (sugar paste) to decorate cakes. You can find many special cutters, leaf molds, and tools in cake decorating shops and most of these can be used successfully with polymer clay. Not all brands of polymer clay are easy to use with these techniques: choose a firm clay that does not have a sticky surface and is strong after baking, because the clay is worked so thin (see page 125). Virtually all the colors used are mixed with translucent clay to simulate translucent flower petals.

Why not make a whole garden's worth of flowers?

6 Roll out pale leaf green clay on the baking parchment very thinly and use the calyx cutter to cut a calyx. Thin and cup it in the same way as the flower.

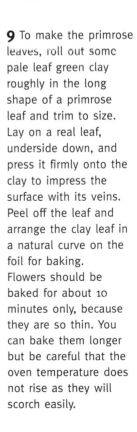

9 To make the primrose leaves, roll out some pale leaf green clay roughly in the long shape of a primrose leaf and trim to size. Lay on a real leaf, underside down, and press it firmly onto the clay to impress the surface with its veins. Peel off the leaf and arrange the clay leaf in a natural curve on the foil for baking. Flowers should be baked for about 10 minutes only, because they are so thin. You can bake them longer but be careful that the oven temperature does not rise as they will scorch easily.

5 Take a 6 in (150mm) length of green wire, using it twisted double if necessary for strength, and bend a little loop in one end. Form a 1/16 in (2mm) ball of golden yellow clay and press this onto the loop. Thread the end of the wire through the center of the flower, emerging from the point of the trumpet end, and pull it through until the ball is pulled into the central hole.

7 Thread the end of the stem through the center of the calyx and pull the calyx up to the the flower. Lightly press the points up round the bottom of the flower.

8 Delicate polymer clay flowers should be baked hanging inside a jar. Fix a wooden skewer across the jar with some scrap clay and hang the flowers from this by making temporary hooks in their stems.

Vessels, Boxes, and Frames

Creating three-dimensional artifacts with polymer clay is one of the most exciting aspects of the craft, and gives wonderful scope for experimenting with decorating techniques. There are many different ways of constructing free-standing objects in polymer clay, and most of the major techniques are covered here.

Painted daisies decorate the finished box.

SIMPLE BOXES

This sequence shows how to make a simple round box using a small essence bottle as the former. You can use clay mixtures of any kind for the box: marbled clay, simulated stones or wood, bone, or ceramic mixtures.

YOU WILL NEED

- *Polymer clay: blue*
- *Roller or pasta machine*
- *Small bottle about 1⅜ in (35mm) in diameter*
- *Foil*
- *Glue*
- *Knife*
- *Blade*
- *Non-stick baking parchment*

1 Cut a piece of foil to fit tightly around the bottle, and glue in place. Roll out some clay, ⅛ in (3mm) thick. Stand the bottle on the clay and cut out the base. Press the base onto the bottom of the bottle, so it sticks.

2 Roll out another ⅛ in (3mm) sheet of clay and cut a strip, 1¾ in (45mm) wide, and long enough to go round the bottle. Lay the bottle on the strip with the base aligned exactly with the strip edge. Roll it up in the strip until the first edge meets the strip again and makes a mark. Cut along the mark, which should give you an exact fit with the two ends butted together.

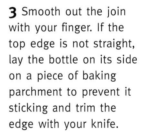

3 Smooth out the join with your finger. If the top edge is not straight, lay the bottle on its side on a piece of baking parchment to prevent it sticking and trim the edge with your knife.

4 Bake the box for 20 to 30 minutes. Allow it to cool until it is lukewarm, then remove it from the bottle. It should slide off the bottle, and you can then remove the foil. It is easier to remove the box when the clay is warm but not too hot.

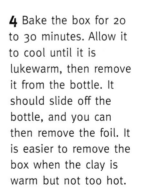

5 To make the lid liner, roll out a ⅛ in (3mm) sheet of clay and invert the box into it, pressing down to make an impression. Use your knife to cut carefully round the inside line and this will give you a disc that will be exactly the diameter of the interior of the box.

USING FORMERS

Once baked, polymer clay is remarkably strong, even when used quite thinly. An ideal way to create vessels, bowls, and boxes is to use a former of some kind as a support while building and then baking the clay. You will find many useful formers in your home: small bottles, (jelly) jam jars, china bowls, matchboxes covered with foil—anything in fact that will survive the low oven baking temperatures. Remember that you will need to remove the former from the clay after baking, so globe-shaped bowls or waisted bottles will be unsuitable.

Cane slices decorate this finished bowl. Use sandpaper to smooth any rough surfaces after baking.

6 To make the lid, you can cut a circle from a decorated sheet of clay or you can make a simple lid for decorating after baking. For the latter, form a 1 in (25mm) ball of clay and press down onto a piece of baking parchment with the pad of your finer until it is slightly larger in diameter than the box.

7 Bake both lid pieces, and then glue the liner centrally onto the inside of the lid. This will give you a tight-fitting lid. You can now decorate the box as you wish and re-bake as necessary. The box should not need inner support for re-baking, but should be handled carefully when hot.

BOWLS

Bowls can be made using a range of china bowls as formers. Here, sections of clay sheet were laid inside a china bowl and the sections smoothed together.

YOU WILL NEED

- *Polymer clay*
- *Roller or pasta machine*
- *Small bowl*
- *Foil*
- *Glue*
- *Knife*
- *Blade*
- *Non-stick baking parchment*

Gently prize out the baked clay bowl while it is still warm. You can also use the outside of a bowl, provided it does not have a foot ring, to make bowls or lampshades. Cane slices can be applied directly to a support bowl to make a patterned polymer clay bowl.

COVERING FORMS

While polymer clay can be used to make forms that are self-supporting, there is a wonderful world of design possibilities if you use the clay to cover forms that then remain inside the clay. Suggestions include glass bottles, jars and paperweights, china vases, blown

A patchwork of jewel-colored canes makes an opulent covering for a pottery bottle.

BOTTLES

This technique uses millefiori canes to cover a pottery bottle. The color of the canes tones with the bottle's glaze, so the top of the bottle was left uncovered to display this effect.

YOU WILL NEED

- *Polymer clay: two toning or contrasting square millefiori canes, about ¼ in (19mm) thick, matching clay for the stopper*
- *Pottery bottle*
- *PVA glue and spreader*
- *Blade*
- *Baking parchment*
- *Small roller*
- *Sandpaper*

1 Cut several slices, about ¹⁄₁₆ in (2mm) thick, from the first cane. Spread glue thinly over the bottle's center to provide a key for the clay slices. Press the slices round the center of the bottle, so that the corners just touch.

2 Now apply slices of the second cane in a row below the first. They should fit neatly into the spaces but you can manipulate them to fit as necessary. Repeat with another row above and continue up the bottle, alternating rows, until you reach the shoulder.

3 When the bottle begins to curve inwards, you will need to manipulate the canes to fit into the smaller diameter. You can either reduce the cane or squeeze each slice into an elongated shape. This forms the top row for this bottle but you can continue up to the top.

4 Cut the canes in half for the bottom row. They should be just longer than the bottle so that they can be neatly turned under the base. Alternatively, you could cover right round the bottom of the bottle.

5 Smooth all the cane slices together evenly, pressing them lightly to push them together and fill any gaps. If you are using a soft clay, lay baking parchment round the bottle to prevent sticking and smooth with a small roller or tool. It is a matter of personal preference whether you want to smooth to a mirror finish or leave the canes more separate with a texture.

eggs, candlesticks and lamp bases, glass lampshades and candle votives, papier maché boxes and bowls. Only use materials that can withstand the baking temperature and avoid plastics, which may give off toxic fumes when baked.

Canes completely cover this glass perfume bottle. The stopper has been covered with canes to match.

6 To make the stopper, form a long cone of clay in a contrast color and push it into the top of the bottle, smoothing the stopper's top. Bake the bottle and the stopper for at least 30 minutes to allow for the pottery absorbing the heat. When the bottle is cool, you can sand to remove any irregularities and buff for a shine.

FRAMES

Frames are easy to cover with cane slices in the same way as the bottle. Alternatively, you can cover frames with rolled out sheets of clay, as shown here. These can then be decorated to create unique pieces for displaying photographs and paintings.

YOU WILL NEED

- *Polymer clay: silver*
- *Frame of metal, wood, or papier maché*
- *Knife*

1 Remove the glass and backing board from the frame to be covered. Roll out a sheet of clay, 1/16 in (2mm) thick and cut out a piece large enough to cover the top of the frame. Press the clay over the frame and trim it along the top edge. Trim the inside edge by running the knife blade along it. Press the clay edges to the back to secure.

2 Cover one of the sides in the same way, leaving excess clay at the corner where the two sheets meet. Cut through both sheets at a mitered angle into the corner. Pull out the excess clay, butt the

join together and smooth it. Repeat for the rest of the frame. You can now decorate the clay with metallics, stamping, flowers, bows, sculptures, faux stones, or with any number of techniques.

POTTING MINIATURE VESSELS

This is a technique that developed out of bead making to give a wonderful means of forming miniature vessels. It is not difficult to learn and with a little practice, you will be able to make miniature pots of all kinds. The technique works for much larger vessels too.

Potting tools: you will need several paintbrush handles, or similar tools, in increasing sizes. They should be round and smooth with a blunt end. I use a ⅛ in (3mm), ³⁄₁₆ in (5mm) and a ¼ in (6mm). A ⅜ in (10mm) and a ½ in (13mm) are used for larger pots.

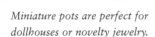

Miniature pots are perfect for dollhouses or novelty jewelry.

MANIPULATING THE CLAY

MINIATURE POT

YOU WILL NEED

- *Polymer clay*
- *Thick tapestry needle*
- *Board or raised work surface*
- *Potting tools as above*
- *Talcum powder*

1 Form a ⅜ in (10mm) thick log of clay and cut a ½ in (13mm) length. Roll the length to make it as round as possible in section if the cutting has squashed it. Stand it on end on your board and pierce exactly into the center with your needle. Push the needle only half way into the clay.

2 With the needle still in the clay, hold it horizontally near the edge of the board so that your hand is lower than the surface and you can keep the needle level. Now press down lightly with the needle as you move your hand from side to side, holding the needle steady. The clay will rotate round the needle and the hole will begin to enlarge.

3 When the hole is big enough, dip the end of the ⅛ in (3mm) paintbrush handle into talcum powder, and insert into the hole. Repeat the action and the hole will enlarge, while the sides thin and the pot grows in diameter.

4 Periodically upend the pot and press down to straighten the rim and compress the pot slightly. (If you find the hole becomes off center, it is best to begin again.) Now continue with a bigger brush handle.

5 When the pot has thin sides and has opened out into a good shape, place it upright on your board and press down inside it with the thickest handle to flatten the bottom. You can now add a handle, mark a rim, or bake it and then make a lid. This basic shape can be used for teacups, flowerpots, storage jars and no end of other miniature pots.

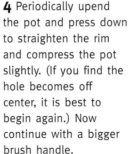

BALLOON VESSELS

These are fun to make and can be used to create vessels, pods, amulets, globes, and many other forms. First a basic pinch pot is formed and the sides are drawn up until the mouth of the vessel can be completely closed, trapping air inside. This gives a resistance against which the sides of the vessel can be pressed in order to smooth and reshape. The piece can then be pierced to re-open it, or left whole to make a pod or amulet. After baking, the piece can be decorated, sanded and polished, painted, or even sawn in half and turned into a box.

Balloon vessels made with marbled clay; every one is unique.

BALLOON JUG

YOU WILL NEED

- *Polymer clay*
- *Scissors*
- *Large tapestry needle*
- *Blunt paintbrush handle or similar tool*

1 Form a 1¼ in (30mm) ball of clay, flatten it a little, and make a hole in the center with your thumbs. With your thumbs in the hole, draw the sides of the pot up around them to form a pot. Keep rotating the pot in your hands, pinching the sides to make them thinner and taller.

2 When the pot is about 1 in (25mm) tall, begin to work the rim inwards by pushing sections towards each other all round and pinching any folds smooth. This will make a neck. When the hole is too small for you to get your finger inside, gather the neck together and press the clay into a point, smoothing any folds. Snip away the top of the point.

3 Roll the balloon in your hands and shape and smooth it into the shape you want. To open the top again, pierce down with a needle and rotate it in the hole to widen the neck. Use the blunt handle to refine and flare the lip.

4 These narrow necked vessels make beautiful ornate bottles when given a stopper, as in the photograph above. Alternatively, you can add a handle: roll out a strip of clay, about the same height as the vessel. Apply one end to the rim, with the rest of the strip lying upwards. Curve this round and down to the base of the vessel and press it on again.

BOXES FROM BAKED SHEETS

This technique shows you how to make boxes from baked sheets of clay. It is particularly useful for making simulated wooden boxes for miniatures; simulated marble boxes for faux stones and pietre dure effects; and any rectangular or square box. These boxes can be fitted with hinged lids (miniature hinges are available from dollhouse suppliers and craft shops).

The finished box is decorated with appliqué flowers (see pages 21 and 48).

BASIC BOX

YOU WILL NEED

- *Polymer clay: turquoise, green, and pearl*
- *Roller or pasta machine*
- *Tracing paper and pencil*
- *Blade*
- *Two ceramic tiles*
- *Sandpaper*
- *Metal ruler or straight edge*
- *Superglue*
- *Foil*
- *Cocktail stick*
- *Set square*

TEMPLATE
Use a photocopier to enlarge by 162%.

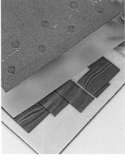

1 Marble the clay colors lightly together and then roll out into a ⅛ in (3mm) thick marbled sheet on the tile. Trace and cut out the templates and lay them onto the clay sheet, keeping the 'grain' of the marbling upright on the front, back, and side pieces. Use a straight blade to cut out the clay pieces, removing the scrap clay from around them.

2 Once all the pieces are cut out, do not remove them from the tile or they will distort. Lay a smooth piece of tracing paper over them all, cover with an upturned tile and bake for about 40 minutes. When the pieces are cool, remove them from the tile and sand them smooth if you wish.

3 Trim the edges of the pieces as necessary for a tight fit, using a metal straight edge and a blade. Apply superglue to the bottom of the box sides. Press these onto the box base, using a set square to ensure they are upright.

4 Glue on the front and back of the box. You can now glue on a hinge for the lid or make a tight fitting lid using the same technique as for the round box on page 62.

TEMPLATE

Base	Front and Back
Sides (cut two)	Top

2⅜ (60mm)

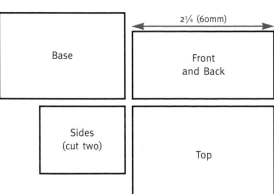

FRAMES

Frames are lovely gifts and you can make a series to frame family portraits.

Simple frames can be made entirely from polymer clay and make lovely gifts. Once the basic frame is made, it can be decorated in many ways. Metallic effects and stamping look particularly good on frames, because they suggest traditional engraved silver frames. Remember that a frame is intended to set off the photograph inside it, so good frame design should not be too gaudy.

If you want to make your frames free-standing, you can tape a triangular sheet of polymer clay to the back so that it will prop up the frame. The all-purpose glue suggested here is not permanent glue for polymer clay so you will be able to separate the frame to replace the picture if you wish.

ROSE FRAME

This little frame is made with copper clay and decorated with simple roses. The frame is cut out using an oval tin lid and an ellipse template but you could use two different sized cutters of any suitable shape.

YOU WILL NEED

- Polymer clay: copper
- Roller or pasta machine
- Ceramic tile
- Oval tin lid or similar object to use as a template
- Knife
- Draughtsman's ellipse template
- Sandpaper
- Photograph to fit the frame
- All-purpose glue

1 Roll the clay into a sheet ⅛ in (3mm) thick and lay it on the tile. Use the tin lid as a guide to cut out two ovals for the frame front and back. Remove the waste clay from around the frame pieces.

2 Choose a suitable sized ellipse for the cut-out in the front of the frame, lay on the template, and cut round it with your knife. Pull away the cut-out portion carefully so that you do not damage the frame front.

3 Decorate the frame front with small roses and leaves (see page 60 for flower techniques). Bake the frame pieces on the tile for 30 minutes. When the pieces are cool, hold the front in place on the back and sand the edges smooth.

4 Position the frame front over the photograph and draw round the outside. Cut out the photograph ¼ in (6mm) outside this line. Glue the photograph lightly to the back of the frame and glue the frame front over it.

Stamped frames brushed with metallic powders imitate fine antique silver and brass.

See also
•
FLOWER TECHNIQUES
PAGE 60-61
USING FORMERS
PAGES 62-65

Flowers and using formers

Clocks are very simple to make in polymer clay and can be decorated in many different ways. Here, a saucer is used as a former for a simple marbled wall clock that is decorated with delicate daisies.

FLOWER CLOCK

You can purchase inexpensive quartz movements from hobby suppliers to fit your polymer clay clock. They are sold with a choice of hands, giving exciting design possibilities. Black filigree hands were chosen here to contrast with the pastel colors of the face. You will need to follow the assembly instructions for your movement, as they may differ from the movement shown here.

MIXTURE

- *Light blue = 8 parts white + 1 part blue*

YOU WILL NEED

- *Polymer clay: white, golden yellow, blue, translucent*
- *Ceramic tile*
- *Knife*
- *Fine sieve*
- *Artists' pastel: crimson*
- *Scrap paper*
- *Paintbrush*
- *Roller or pasta machine*
- *A saucer with a smooth underside*
- *Drinking straw or brush protector*
- *Clock movement for a wall clock*

1 You will need five daisies altogether. For each daisy, form a ⅛ in (3mm) ball of white clay and press it onto the tile to make a base disc. Form a ¼ in (6mm) log of white clay and flatten it into an oval cross section. Cut and apply about ten slices for petals to the disc (see appliqué flowers on page 48).

2 Form a ³⁄₁₆ in (5mm) log of golden yellow clay and cut a ³⁄₁₆ in (5mm) length. Roll into a ball and flatten into a small disc. Push this hard against the mesh of the strainer to texture the surface. Use your knife to press it onto the center of the daisy without flattening the texture. Make ten separate petals, slicing and applying them directly to the tile.

3 Rub a little crimson pastel onto the paper and brush onto the tips of the daisy petals. Flick up some of the daisy petals for a more natural look. Bake the daisies and the separate petals on the tile for 20 minutes. Allow to cool before removing them from the tile.

4 Marble together the white, light blue, and transparent clays. You will need about half a block of each color. Roll out to make a sheet about ⅛ in (3mm) thick and large enough to cover the saucer. Lay the sheet over the saucer and trim round with your knife to make the clock face.

5 Use a drinking straw or brush protector to cut a hole in the center of the clock. This needs to be large enough to allow the clock's spindle to be inserted.

6 Press the baked separate petals all round the clock face, from the one o'clock through to the ten o'clock position. Press a baked daisy onto the twelve o'clock position and then press the remaining four daisies in a loose 'S' shape down the clock face.

7 Bake the clock for 30 minutes. Allow to cool, then ease off the saucer. Insert the clock movement spindle through the hole, cutting it wider if necessary.

8 Screw the spindle screw down onto the clock face to hold the clock movement firmly onto the back of the clock. Do not screw down too hard or you may damage the clay.

9 Fit the hands onto the spindle and screw down the holding screw to keep them in place. The clock can be hung on the wall using the integral hanger built into the back of the clock movement.

COMBINING TECHNIQUES

VARIATIONS

- *There are endless variations possible when making polymer clay clocks. You can decorate the clock face using any of the techniques in this book: try using metal powders for a brass-effect Celtic clock*
- *Use a different shaped former for the basic clock face—for example, a foil-covered square box lid will give a pleasing square clock*

SUE HEASER
Rajasthani Woman
Brilliant colors, caning, and textile simulation combine with a sculpted face to make a unique brooch.

ALEXANDRA BLYTHE
Parrots
Tiny polymer clay parrots in a metal cage are sculpted at the popular miniature scale of 1:12.

KATHERINE DEWEY
*Bas-relief egg
'Bright Moon'*
A bas-relief fairy is sculpted onto a dark blue clay egg for a hauntingly beautiful piece. Translucent clay in the bas-relief provides subtle color variations and a porcelain effect.

LYNDA STRUBLE
Faerie
This enchanting little creature is 9 in (23cm) tall. She is sculpted polymer clay with a posable wire frame for the body and has fabric clothes. Her lively pose is truly delightful.

MARIE SEGAL
GREEN MAN
*A sculpted face is surrounded
by intricate cane slices
to create a wonderful
traditional image
reminiscent of
medieval bosses.*

MARIA GOWER
ROSE JEWELRY
*These exquisite sculpted
roses are virtually
indistinguishable from
the real thing and use
polymer clay worked
extremely thin. Delicate
graded colors enhance
the realism.*

SCULPTING

Sculpting is a natural use
for polymer clay and the
added dimension of colored
clays gives superlative
results.

SUE HEASER
BIRD BROOCH
*The delicate natural
colors of a blue tit
make a delightful
subject for a
sculpted brooch.
Touches of acrylic
paint accent
the piece.*

SUE HEASER
MINIATURE DOLLS
*Sculpted polymer clay dollhouse
dolls in 1:12 scale are clothed in
fabric with mohair for hair. The
dolls are all posable and make
perfect occupants for a dollhouse.*

SIMPLE TECHNIQUES

When modeling simple animals in polymer clay, use pictures of real animals as a guide and your results will be far more realistic. You can also use other polymer clay techniques to enhance your models; for example, use cane slices for turtle shells, loops of coiled clay for sheep wool, and metallic powders for gleaming fish.

Gold clay gives the finished owl a mellow sheen. Try using different browns or marbled clay for variety.

OWL

Owls are great favorites with many people and these instructions are for an owl 1½ in (40 mm) tall. You can enlarge or reduce the measurements to make a whole family of owls of different sizes.

YOU WILL NEED

- Polymer clay: golden yellow, beige, gold (or light brown), black
- Ceramic tile
- Knife
- Large tapestry needle
- Gloss varnish

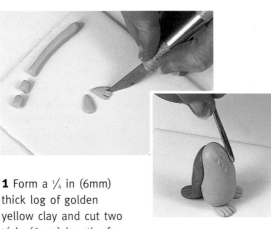

1 Form a ¼ in (6mm) thick log of golden yellow clay and cut two ¼ in (6mm) lengths for the feet. Shape these into balls and then teardrops, and press them down onto the tile with the points angled together at the back as shown. Use your knife to make three cuts in each for the toes.

2 Form a ¾ in (20mm) ball of beige clay and another, the same size, of gold. Shape them into ovals and press together to make the body. Pull out the base of the gold half to form a tail at the back and press the body down onto the feet. Use the eye of the needle to mark feathers on the front of the body.

3 Form two ½ in (13mm) balls of gold clay, shape each into an elongated teardrop and flatten into a wing shape. Press one onto each side of the body, with the points trailing backwards to the tail. Form a ¾ in (19mm) ball of gold for the head and press onto the top of the body.

4 Press two ⅛ in (3mm) balls of beige clay onto the face for the eye patches. Form two 3⁄16 in (5mm) balls of gold clay into pointed teardrops and press one on above each eye for the 'ears'. Press on a tiny point of yellow for the beak, and mark nostrils with your needle. Make holes for eye sockets and fill each with a 1⁄16 in (2mm) black ball. Bake on the tile for 20 minutes and, when cool, varnish the eyes to make them sparkle.

MODEL ANIMALS

The simple, smiling face of the caterpillar makes it particularly appealing to children. Try reversing the mouth for the occasional glum personality!

If you are one of those people who instinctively begins to create a little creature whenever they are given a piece of clay or dough, then you will find modeling animals with polymer clay an enchanting occupation. The bright colors just ask to be turned into piglets and owls, penguins and toucans. The soft surface can be beautifully textured for feathers, fur, and scales while marbling techniques give even more effects.

When building animal models, you need to start at the bottom and work upwards. The feet are nearly always the first to be modeled, followed by the body and upper limbs or wings, and finally the head and features.

CATERPILLAR

Little creepy crawly models delight children, and this cheerful caterpillar can be made in a wonderful variety of color schemes, ranging from the tasteful to the bizarre! Try using glow-in-the-dark clay for a night-time display of glow-worms.

MATERIALS

- Polymer clay: yellow, pearl green, fluorescent pink, black
- Ceramic tile
- Knife
- Brush protector or drinking straw
- Blunt tapestry needle
- Gloss varnish

1 Form a ½ in (13mm) thick log of pearl green clay and cut seven ½ in (13mm) lengths. Form another log, ¼ in (6mm) thick, of yellow and cut seven ¼ in (6mm) lengths. Roll all the pieces into balls. Flatten a yellow ball and press onto a larger green ball. Roll to smooth together and shape into a pointed oval to make the tail.

2 Roll together the remaining balls of green and yellow clay in the same way to make two-color balls. Press one onto the blunt end of the tail to make the first segment of the caterpillar body, keeping the yellow side downwards. Press on the remaining balls, with the last three stacked upright with the yellow side to the front.

3 Form a ¾ in (19mm) ball of green clay for the head and press onto the top of the body. Slightly flatten a ¼ in (6mm) log of pink clay and cut slices from it for the feet, applying them to both sides of the body with your knife (see Appliqué on page 48).

4 Press the end of a brush protector into the lower face to make a smiley mouth. Make two holes for eye sockets and fill each with a tiny ball of black. Bake the model on the tile for 20 minutes and, when cool, varnish the eyes.

RELIEF FACES

Sculpting the human face is one of the more challenging techniques with any modeling or sculpting medium but is a skill that is extremely useful to master. The obvious uses of face sculpture are for figurines and dolls, but human faces make beautiful jewelry as well. These haunting brooches are sculptures of women from Rajasthan in Northwest India, although the basic techniques can be adapted to sculpt faces of all ages and

The completed brooch combines sculpting, caning, and painting.

SCULPTING

SCULPTED BROOCH

YOU WILL NEED

- *Polymer clay: brown, black, crimson, red, yellow, gold*
- *Ceramic tile*
- *Knife with a curved blade*
- *Smooth round pencil*
- *Blunt stainless steel tool for smoothing*
- *Large tapestry needle*
- *Soft paintbrush*
- *Darning needle*
- *Roller*
- *Denatured alcohol (methylated spirits)*
- *Acrylic paints: brown, black, white, crimson*
- *Fine paintbrush*
- *Matt varnish*
- *Brooch back or magnet*
- *Epoxy glue or superglue*

VARIATIONS

- *Always work from photographs or life to get the best results*
- *Add elaborate hairstyles and hats for more exotic looks*

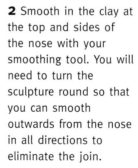

1 Form a 1 in (25mm) ball of brown clay, roll it into an egg shape and press it down onto the tile. Press the side of a smooth pencil horizontally onto the center of the face to indent it. Form a ³/₁₆ in (5mm) ball of brown clay and shape it into a teardrop. Press onto the center of the face for the nose.

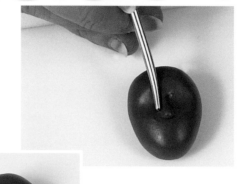

2 Smooth in the clay at the top and sides of the nose with your smoothing tool. You will need to turn the sculpture round so that you can smooth outwards from the nose in all directions to eliminate the join.

3 Make an indentation on either side of the mouth area with your tapestry needle. The grooves need to run down from the outside of the nose to the chin. Use the knife to make a horizontal mouth cut between the grooves, about ¹/₈ in (3mm) below the nose.

4 Press a vertical line onto the center of the top lip. Use your tapestry needle to smooth upwards from the mouth cut to shape the upper lip. Now make a horizontal indentation ¹/₁₆ in (2mm) below the mouth cut with your tapestry needle. Smooth away any sharp edges.

races. Your sculpting will be far more successful if you study faces and photographs to use as reference for your work.

The tools for small-scale sculpture are extremely simple and the basic requirements are listed below. If you enjoy sculpting, you may find that you want to add a ball tool, or other sculpting tools, to this basic list but they are by no means essential.

It is important to choose a smoothable clay for sculpting, so check the table on page 125.

Every brooch is unique when sculpted by hand. If you sculpt a face that you particularly like, make a push mold of it so that you can duplicate the original (see page 56).

5 Brush over the face with a soft paintbrush to smooth the surface. Pinch the chin to accentuate it if necessary. Lightly draw in the suggestion of eyes with the tapestry needle. Roll out some black clay and apply a sheet over the top of the head for the hair. Mark a parting and texture the hair with the darning needle. Pierce two tiny holes for nostrils.

6 Roll out the crimson clay to make a thin sheet 7 in (175mm) long and ³/₄ in (19mm) wide. Make a simple cane using red and yellow (see page 36) and apply slices to one edge of the strip. Roll again to smooth in the cane slices.

7 Wrap the sheet around the head and trim it to fit, tucking it around the back of the head. Form the front into an attractive drape around the face.

8 Form a ¹/₃₂ in (1mm) thick log of gold clay and press it onto the edge of the sheet all round the front of the face. Make a typical Rajasthani nose ring by forming a thin ring of gold clay and pressing it onto the side of the nose. Apply tiny slices round the ring for decoration. Bake the sculpture on the tile for 20-30 minutes and allow to cool.

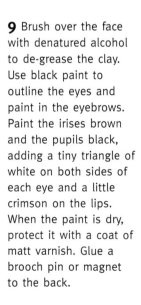

9 Brush over the face with denatured alcohol to de-grease the clay. Use black paint to outline the eyes and paint in the eyebrows. Paint the irises brown and the pupils black, adding a tiny triangle of white on both sides of each eye and a little crimson on the lips. When the paint is dry, protect it with a coat of matt varnish. Glue a brooch pin or magnet to the back.

Using Armatures

Armatures serve several useful purposes in free-standing polymer clay sculpture. Firstly, they provide a frame upon which to build the clay. Secondly, they cut down the quantity of clay required so that the resulting sculpture is lighter and bakes thoroughly in a shorter time. Thirdly, they support the sculpture after baking, which is particularly important with the more fragile clays. Foil and wire are ideal materials for polymer clay armatures because they are inert and can remain inside the sculpture without causing problems. Wire should always be galvanized or non-rusting.

SUFFOLK BROWNIE

This figurine is a mythical creature of British folklore.

YOU WILL NEED

- Polymer clay: beige (or any neutral color), copper, dark brown, white, light brown, gold, leaf green, stone clays, scrap clay, smoothable flesh clay

- *Tracing paper, pencil*
- *Medium gauge wire*
- *Wire cutting pliers*
- *Knife with curved blade*
- *Roller*
- *Aluminum foil*
- *Large tapestry needle*
- *Blunt stainless steel tool*
- *Soft paintbrush*
- *Darning needle*
- *Roller or pasta machine*
- *Denatured alcohol (methylated spirits)*
- *Acrylic paint: blue, brown, black, white, crimson*
- *Fine paintbrush*
- *Matt varnish*
- *Artists' pastel: carmine, burnt umber, burnt sienna, yellow ocher*
- *Fine strainer or sieve*
- *Ceramic tile*
- *Epoxy glue or superglue*

TEMPLATE
Enlarge on a photocopier 189% so that the height is 7 in (178mm).

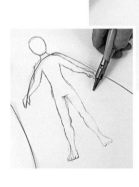

1 Enlarge the template and make a tracing. Cut a 20 in (50cm) length of wire, bend it in half, and hold it over the tracing. Twist the wire together at the neck and waist, leaving the wire opened out into loops for the head and upper body. Cut a second piece of wire long enough to go from one hand, right through the shoulders, to the other hand.

2 Tear off strips of foil and wrap them round the body and head. Push the arm wire through the foil covering the body and then wrap more foil to secure it. Squeeze the foil to compact it and shape it so that it is a little thinner all over than the traced template. Do not cover the limbs with foil.

FIGURINES

Figurines are particularly successful in polymer clay: the excellent specialist doll and flesh clays give realistic flesh tones, while the rich variety of colored clays can be used with textile techniques to clothe the figure. The clay can be baked repeatedly so that each stage is hardened before proceeding to the next. Finally, the clay is a perfect painting surface so delicate features can be added with acrylic paint to give startlingly lifelike effects.

The following sequence shows you how to make a 7 in (178mm) tall figurine using a wire and foil armature. The part of the

3 Roll beige or scrap clay into a sheet about ¹⁄₁₆ in (2mm) thick and cut into strips 1 in (25mm) wide. Wrap these around the foil until the body is completely covered. Push the clay and the foil beneath into shape, to match the template outline. Add extra clay to shape the figure and smooth the joins.

4 Cover the head and neck in the same way as the torso, but using flesh clay. Apply an overlay of flesh clay to the front of the chest. Form a ½ in (13mm) thick log of beige clay and cut two 1⅛ in (28mm) lengths for the upper arms. Thread these onto the arm wires and smooth into the shoulders.

Forearms

5 Form a ⅜ in (10mm) log of flesh clay and cut two 1½ in (38mm) lengths. Round one end of each and thin the clay into a wrist ½ in (13mm) from the rounded end. Press the resulting ball ends onto your work surface for the hands. Cut a V-shape out of each and mark fingers with your knife. Smooth and round the fingers with the tapestry needle.

6 Mark nails with the eye of the tapestry needle. Slice under each hand with your knife to remove it from the work surface. Mark details on the inside of the hand with your needle. Curve the hands into a natural shape and thin the wrist.

7 Trim the arm wires to just shorter than the base of the fingers. Trim the forearms to length and thread them onto the arm wires, smoothing the join with the upper arms. Bend the wire at the elbows and refine the shape.

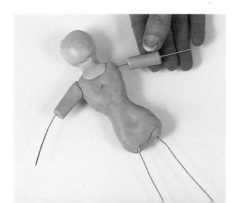

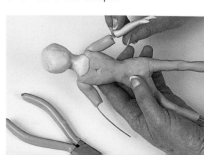

Folklore is a rich source of ideas for sculpted figures. You can also draw inspiration from everyday life, history, or fantasy and science fiction.

torso that is hidden under the clothes is made with beige clay, while a firm, smoothable flesh clay is used for the head, hands, and feet. When sculpting the basic figure, you will achieve much greater realism if you refer to photographs of the human figure as you work. Models in clothes catalogues, especially those modeling swimwear, are particularly useful, or you can make your own sketches from life.

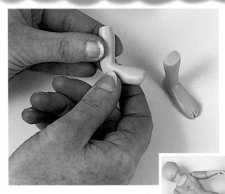

Legs

8 Form a ½ in (13mm) log of flesh clay and cut two 2 in (50mm) lengths. Round one end of each and then pull down a heel ¾ in (19mm) from the rounded end. Press the foot onto the work surface, mark toes with the knife and shape the foot. Thin the ankle and shape the back of the calf, reversing, shaping for the second foot.

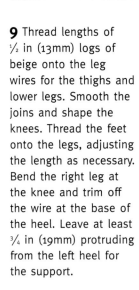

9 Thread lengths of ½ in (13mm) logs of beige onto the leg wires for the thighs and lower legs. Smooth the joins and shape the knees. Thread the feet onto the legs, adjusting the length as necessary. Bend the right leg at the knee and trim off the wire at the base of the heel. Leave at least ¾ in (19mm) protruding from the left heel for the support.

Face

10 Sculpt the face following the instructions for faces on page 76, using flesh clay. Form small teardrops of flesh clay, flatten them, and apply to the side of the head with the points up, to make elfin ears. Smooth the clay towards the face and indent the center. Lay the figure on a baking sheet and adjust his pose as necessary. Support hands and feet with foil and bake for 45 minutes.

Shirt

11 Roll out a ⅟₁₆ in (2mm) thick sheet of copper clay. Cut a piece big enough to cover the top front of the figure. Use a knife or a pair of sharp scissors to cut the clay to size with a V-shape cut out for the neck. Cut out the armholes but leave the sides generously wide.

12 Cut another sheet of copper clay for the back, lay it on, and trim to size. Trim and then overlap the side seams and smooth neatly to suggest a stitched seam. The shirt should be long enough to reach to the hips.

When sculpting figures, an active pose such as this one gives added impact: the Brownie looks poised to take a step at any moment.

13 Make two strips of lace (see page 52) and gather round the wrists for frilled cuffs. Cut two sleeves in the shape shown, long enough to reach from the top of the shoulder to the cuff. Press onto the figure, using a modeling tool to smooth, and drape the clay around the arms. Press the underarm seam together and apply extra strips of clay for cuffs.

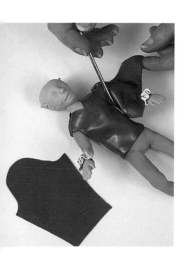

Breeches
14 Roll out a ¹⁄₁₆ in (2mm) thick sheet of dark brown clay. Cut out two pieces in the shape shown, long enough to reach from the waist to mid-calf. Lay one piece round the figure's left leg, with the join up the inside leg, trim to fit, and smooth the seam together. Repeat with the second leg piece, trimming the center body seam and pressing it together.

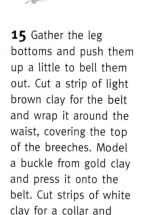

15 Gather the leg bottoms and push them up a little to bell them out. Cut a strip of light brown clay for the belt and wrap it around the waist, covering the top of the breeches. Model a buckle from gold clay and press it onto the belt. Cut strips of white clay for a collar and press on over the raw edge at the neck.

Hair
16 Roll out a sheet of gold clay for the hair and cut pieces to fit over the head, building them up to make the head a good shape. Use a needle to texture the clay and feather the ends to look like hair.

Hat
17 Roll out a ¹⁄₁₆ in (2mm) sheet of leaf green clay and cut out two pointed pieces as shown. Press the pieces together along the front and back joins to make a hat and turn the bottom edge up for a brim. Press onto the figure's head.

SCULPTING TIPS

Keep your hands very clean when using flesh clays—they pick up dust and dirt easily.

Air bubbles can sometimes occur when baking large pieces. Air, trapped in the foil armature, expands on heating and pushes up the clay surface in a large, unsightly mound. To prevent this, pierce through into the foil with a darning needle at unobtrusive points before baking. This will allow any trapped air to escape.

If you enjoy sewing, you can make the clothes from fabric instead of clay.

The finished Brownie stands poised on his rock. This basic figure design can be varied to give many different sculptures.

Painting

18 Bake the figure again for 20 minutes, propping up as necessary to prevent the clothes from being crushed. When the figure is cool, paint the face (see page 77) giving the Brownie blue eyes. Use a thin wash of crimson paint for lips and carmine pastel for the cheeks.

Base

19 Form a base of scrap clay, approximately 4 in (100mm) by 3 in (75mm), and 2 in (50m) high. Roll out some stone clay and cover the scrap clay, shaping it to suggest rocks and boulders. Use other stone-colored clays to make pebbles and add more rocks.

20 Soften some leaf green clay and press it through the sieve to make moss. Scrape the 'moss' off the sieve and press onto the rocks. Rub both browns and the ocher pastels onto scrap paper and apply the resulting powder with a brush onto the base to suggest lichens.

21 Place the base on a tile and press the baked feet of the figurine onto it to impress the soft base with the shape of the feet. The wire support in the left heel will make a deep hole in the base. Bake the base for 45 minutes. When it is cool, glue the

feet to the rocks, with the wire support inserted into the hole, to stabilize the figure.

NATURAL HISTORY SUBJECTS

Natural history subjects are extremely successful when sculpted in polymer clay, because the clay's mixable colors and fine texture give so much scope for imitating nature. This heron ornament is at the popular miniature scale of 1:12, or one inch to one foot, but you can sculpt at any scale you wish.

HERON ORNAMENT

YOU WILL NEED

- Polymer clay: white, gray, black, golden yellow, leaf green
- Tracing paper and pencil
- Fine wire—about 5 - 6½ ft (1.5-2m)
- Needle or needle tool
- Fine-pointed tweezers
- Wooden base (or a large pebble)
- Polymer clay miniature flowers, plants, and rocks (optional)
- Acrylic paint: black
- Gloss varnish

MIXTURES

- Pale gray = 4 parts white + 1 part gray
- Dark gray = 1 part black + 1 part gray
- Pale yellow = 1 part golden yellow + 1 part white
- Creamy white = white + trace of yellow + trace of leaf green
- Green blends for the base: add varying quantities of yellow and/or white clay to leaf green to make several different shades of green

TEMPLATE
The template is a 1:12 scale drawing and is shown actual size. If you wish to draw your own template, you will need the body measurements of a full-size bird, which are usually given in bird guides. Divide every measurement by 12 and use the resulting figures to draw your template.

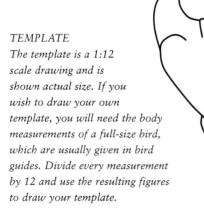

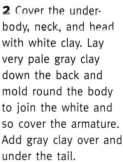

Armature
1 Cut the wire into several short lengths. Start with the beak by folding a length in half to make a sharp point. Use the template as a guide and bend and wrap the wire to form a wire skeleton. When beginning each new piece of wire, simply twist it around the armature to secure.

2 Cover the under-body, neck, and head with white clay. Lay very pale gray clay down the back and mold round the body to join the white and so cover the armature. Add gray clay over and under the tail.

When sculpting for realism, always refer to photographs or illustrations of the original whether it is a bird, animal, fish, tree, plant, or even a house, or a plate of food. This will give you far superior results than if you try to rely on memory.

The base for the heron is finished with baked polymer clay plants, flowers, and rocks but you can use any suitable items provided they will withstand the baking temperature.

Water plants such as iris and ferns are ideal for enhancing the wetland theme of the base.

SCULPTING

Wings

3 The wings are built up in a series of layers. First form two large wing-shaped pieces in black clay and lay along the sides of the body and over the tail. Lay smaller wing-shaped pieces of dark gray over the black at the ends of the wings, allowing the black to show at the edges. Lay a third wing-shaped layer of gray over the whole wing, leaving the black visible along the front and lower edge.

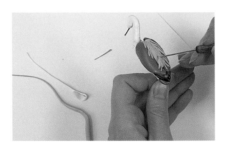

4 Form a $\frac{1}{32}$ in (1mm) thick log of very pale gray and flatten this along its length. Cut into lengths of $\frac{3}{8}$ - $\frac{3}{4}$ in (10-20mm) and apply these to the back to suggest long feathers. Use the needle to texture them and work them in. Repeat with white for the breast feathers.

Head

5 Form a $\frac{1}{32}$ in (1mm) thick log of black, flatten it, and apply $\frac{3}{16}$ in (5mm) lengths to the front for the throat markings. The 'mask' above the eyes is a $\frac{1}{16}$ in (2mm) black log, flattened and applied in the same way.

6 Form a $\frac{1}{8}$ in (3mm) thick log of pale yellow clay, about $\frac{1}{2}$ in (13mm) long, and point one end. Push the wide end onto the beak wire, pressing it firmly onto the face. Squeeze the beak to the correct size, removing excess clay at the pointed end. Make two eye sockets with a blunt point and fill each with a tiny ball of pale yellow. Pierce the center of each and insert an even smaller ball of black clay.

The finished heron in his naturalistic setting would make a wonderful gift for a wildlife enthusiast.

Legs

7 Mold creamy white clay over the leg wires to the length required, leaving at least 2 in (50mm) of bare wire protruding. Insert two short lengths of wire into the back of the head to form the crest feathers. Hold the bird by the leg wires and, starting at the head, use the needle tool to inscribe feathers over the whole bird. Use the tweezers to define wing tips and leg ridges.

8 Bake the bird for 20-30 minutes, hanging it upside-down by the exposed leg wires from the oven shelf. Spread craft glue onto the base and cover it with a shallow mound made from a blend of several different leaf greens to give a mottled effect. Trim the baked heron's leg wires to length and push these into the mound to fix the bird in position. Lay toes of creamy white on the green base around the bottom of each leg.

Base

9 Texture the surface of the green base with the tweezers to suggest grass. Add pre-made polymer clay miniature plants and flowers if you wish, and press on a marbled rock or a few pebbles. Bake again for 20-30 minutes. Paint the wire head plumes black and varnish the surface of the eye.

LINDA GOFF
DUCK AND OWL PINS
The native images of northwest America were the inspiration behind these unusual and appealing pins. Wire, metallic powders, and texturing all add to the final result.

SUE HEASER
CHINESE-STYLE DISC BEAD
The delicate images of Chinese brush painting are used on a stone-effect polymer clay disc bead. Muted colors and a toning silk cord add to the impact.

MIKE BUESSELER
LEAF PIN
The delicate tracery of a real dicentra leaf has been impressed into lavender tinted pearl clay to make this glorious pin. Interference powder and texturing complete the piece.

SUE HEASER
GILDED CLOCK
Celtic designs embellish a polymer clay clock that looks convincingly like opulent metal. The design was inscribed into the soft verdigris-colored clay and metallic powders brushed over.

DIANE DUNVILLE
MOON GLOW LAMP
Texturing, carving, and gold leaf were used to embellish this superb lamp. Translucent clay was wrapped around a former to make the lamp and then layers of colored translucent clay were applied to create the imagery.

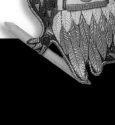

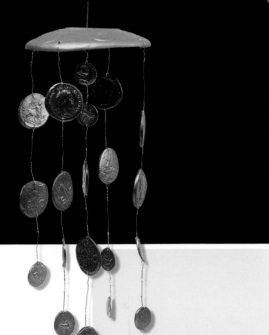

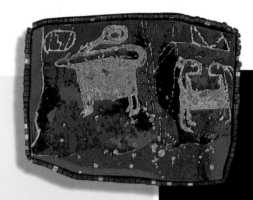

GWEN GIBSON
PETROGLYPH PIN
This technique was developed by the artist and involves clay collages of etched and painted Aboriginal images on a distressed surface. The edge is framed with painted seed beads.

SUE HEASER
COIN MOBILE
A shower of glittering polymer clay coins simulates a Roman hoard of gold and silver. Metallic powders applied to soft clay suggest real metal.

Decoration & Embellishment

Polymer clay can be decorated and embellished in a wonderful variety of ways. The results are often so different that it is hard to believe that they are made from the same material.

SUE HEASER
STAMPED BROOCH & BUTTONS
Stamping and metallic powders are natural companions and make wonderful jewelry.

SUE HEASER
CELTIC HAIR ORNAMENT
The Gibson photo transfer enameling technique is used here to create a striking hair ornament. The plaited clay border has been brushed with metallic powder.

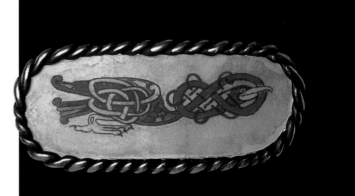

STAMPING

Stamping gives endless possibilities for decorating brooches and buttons.

Man has been decorating clay with stamps since prehistoric times and it is a perfect way of repeating a motif in the soft surface. Polymer clay takes stamped impressions very well and the technique can be combined with other surface techniques, such as powders and paint, to give even more variety.

USING PURCHASED STAMPS

There is an enormous range of commercial rubber stamps available for stamping ink onto paper, and these can be used to great effect with polymer clay. The best results come from stamps with fairly high relief and clear designs.

Stamping polymer clay is simple: smear the clay surface lightly with talcum powder to prevent

USING METALLIC POWDERS

YOU WILL NEED

- *Polymer clay*
- *Ceramic tile*
- *Scrap paper*
- *Metallic powders*
- *Talcum powder*
- *Rubber stamps*

1 To make a stamped pendant or brooch, form a ball of clay and press it down onto the tile to make a circular disc, about ⅛ in (3mm) thick. Sprinkle metallic powder onto paper to make a thin layer. Press the rubber stamp onto the powder several times so that the raised surfaces are evenly covered, and press firmly onto the clay. You can use a smaller stamp to decorate the edge in the same way.

2 To highlight the relief after stamping, first make a disc of clay, dust it lightly with talcum powder, and stamp it. Rub metallic powder onto your finger and brush over the surface of the clay to coat only the raised areas. The two discs at the front show the contrasting techniques using the same stamp.

USING EMBOSSING POWDERS

Embossing powders work very well with polymer clay, because they require heat to melt and set them and the clay baking temperature achieves this perfectly. They can be applied all over the stamped surface, or only in the recessed areas, as in this example.

YOU WILL NEED

- *Polymer clay: copper*
- *Ceramic tile*
- *Talcum powder*
- *Stamp*
- *Embossing powder: verdigris*
- *Paintbrush*

1 Stamp the clay as described above and bake on the tile for 20 minutes. When it is cool, use the paintbrush to brush embossing powder into the recessed areas.

2 Bake again for 10 minutes, or until the embossing powder melts and bubbles. Remove from the oven and cool. The powder will have melted into a glassy infill, looking rather like enamel.

sticking and press the stamp firmly onto the clay. It is best to work on a ceramic tile so that the clay can be baked on the tile without moving it.

See page 59 for instructions on using stamps with gold clay.

MAKING YOUR OWN STAMPS

While it is fun to use purchased stamps with polymer clay, it is even better to make your own out of the clay itself. Polymer clay can take highly detailed impressions from many objects around your home, such as jewelry, engraved cutlery, or any other textured surfaces. These impressions are then baked to make stamps. Alternatively, you can inscribe your own motifs on stamps as in the sequence here.

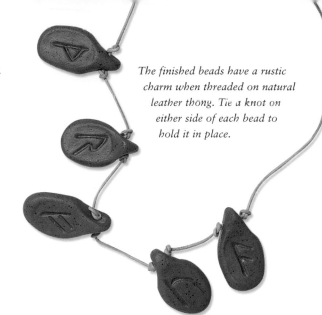

The finished beads have a rustic charm when threaded on natural leather thong. Tie a knot on either side of each bead to hold it in place.

STAMPS FROM INSCRIPTIONS

This is a very simple technique but one that can be used in many exciting ways. Here, inscribed runes have been used to make simple pendant beads but you could also use designs such as Egyptian hieroglyphs, Chinese characters or signs of the Zodiac.

These runes are letters from an early Anglo Saxon alphabet used in the 3rd century AD. They were considered to have magical significance and were often inscribed on stones and jewelry.

YOU WILL NEED

- *Polymer clay: scrap clay for the stamps, stone effect for the beads*
- *Roller*
- *Ceramic tile*
- *Blunt modeling tool or tapestry needle*
- *Talcum powder*
- *Paintbrush*
- *Superglue*
- *Darning needle*
- *Metallic paste*

1 Roll out a strip of clay on the tile, about 1/16 in (2mm) thick. With the photograph as a guide, use the blunt tool to inscribe the runes firmly into the clay. You may need to go over each stroke again to make a good indented line. Bake on the tile for 20 minutes.

2 When the strip is cool, brush over it liberally with talcum powder. Form some balls of scrap clay and press one firmly onto each inscribed rune. Bake the stamps, plus some logs of clay for handles. When cool, glue the handles to the back of the stamps.

3 Form some 1/2 in (13mm) balls of stone clay and shape them into ovals. Pinch the tops and pierce horizontally. Brush the surface with talcum powder. Rub metallic paste onto the raised surface of each stamp and impress the beads; the paste will accentuate the stamped rune. These beads make unusual jewelry when strung on a leather thong.

METALLIC POWDERS AND LEAFS

Metallic effects on polymer clay give truly magical results. The clay surface readily accepts both powders and metallic leaf, to produce effects that dazzle.

Metallic effects on polymer clay give truly magical results. The clay surface readily accepts both powders and metallic leaf to produce effects that dazzle.

METALLIC AND PEARLESCENT POWDERS

These powders are brushed onto the soft clay where they stick to produce a coating that simulates metal. Many different powders are available: gold, silver, copper, bronze, antique gold, metallic colors, pearlescent colors, and two-tone interference colors. Be careful when using powders, because the particles can cause irritation if inhaled. Apply sparingly and work in a well-ventilated area, or use a dust mask.

CELTIC KNOT HAIR ORNAMENT

Knotwork designs from illuminated manuscripts are the inspiration for this hair ornament. You should be able to find books containing these designs to give you further ideas.

YOU WILL NEED

- *Polymer clay: black*
- *Metallic powder: blue, green, purple, violet*
- *Soft paintbrush*
- *Large hairclip or barrette*
- *Superglue*
- *Gloss varnish*

METAL LEAF BEADS

Spirals of silver leaf decorate these black beads to create an opulent effect.

2 Using the paintbrush, brush the metallic powders onto the clay, changing color every 2 in (50mm) or so, and brushing the powder round the sides as well. Bake the knot for 20 minutes and, while it is still warm and flexible, glue it to the curved surface of the hairclip. Varnish the powder with gloss varnish to protect it.

YOU WILL NEED

- *Polymer clay: black*
- *Roller or pasta machine*
- *Baking parchment*
- *Soft paintbrush*
- *Imitation silver leaf*
- *Knife*
- *Darning needle*
- *Gloss varnish*

1 Roll out a ¼ in (6mm) thick log of black clay, at least 18 in (450mm) long. Using the photograph as a guide, and starting with the bottom central loop at the center of the log, weave the two ends until you have recreated the knot. Trim the log and press the two ends together to complete.

METAL LEAF

True gold leaf is extremely costly but the imitation gold leaf, or 'Dutch Leaf', is an excellent alternative to use with polymer clay. It is available in gold, silver, and copper, as well as mixed colors. Imitation leaf should always be varnished to prevent tarnishing.

When metal leaf is applied to a sheet of clay and then rolled in, it will shatter into a beautiful surface pattern.

ARTISTS' PASTELS

Powder color can be brushed onto polymer clay to give wonderfully subtle effects, the best kind to use being artists' soft pastels. They create beautiful graded areas of color with no hard edges, and are perfect for blushing flower petals, browning miniature food, or delicate color effects on jewelry.

If the piece is likely to undergo wear and tear, as in the case of jewelry, you will need to varnish it for protection.

1 Roll out a ¹⁄₁₆ in (2mm) thick sheet of black clay on the baking parchment. Lift a sheet of leaf onto the clay, helping it into place with the paintbrush. Tear away the excess for future use. Roll over the surface of the leaf with your roller until the leaf becomes crazed.

2 Form several balls of black clay for beads. Cut ¹⁄₈ in (3mm) wide strips from the sheet and wrap these round the balls in a spiral pattern. Roll the balls lightly to work the strips in and they will appear to have shattered swirls of silver leaf spiraling round them. Pierce, bake, and varnish to protect the leaf.

ADDING PASTEL COLOR

YOU WILL NEED

- *Artists' pastels*
- *Plain, white paper*
- *Soft paintbrush*
- *Gloss or matt varnish as required*

To apply graded tints to color the unbaked petals of polymer clay flowers, rub the colors onto the paper to make powder. Use the brush to scoop up a light coating of the powder. Stroke the color gently onto the petals, applying it sparingly, and building up layers for a deeper shade.

Miniature polymer clay food is transformed by the use of pastel color. Pies and bread can be browned, apples blushed, and roast meat pinked. Burnt sienna is a particularly useful color—it is a reddish brown that perfectly imitates browning on baked food. Combine it with burnt umber and yellow ocher for variety. Gloss varnish over the browning makes food look glazed or oily.

See also
•
STAMPING
PAGES 88-89
METALLIC POWDERS
PAGES 90-91

Stamping and metallic powders

Stamping combines superbly with metallic powders to give polymer clay wonderful highlighted surfaces. This project shows you how to make your own stamps from replica coins, to create a shower of polymer clay coins for a spectacular mobile.

ROMAN COIN MOBILE

The coins used here are replicas made from real Roman coins but you could use any type of obsolete coins, medals, or even buttons to make the mobile.

YOU WILL NEED

- *Polymer clay: any color clay for the stamps, black, gold (optional)*
- *Four or five different replica coins*
- *Ceramic tile*
- *Soft paintbrush*
- *Talcum powder*
- *Baking parchment*
- *Metallic powder: gold, silver, bronze, copper*
- *Darning needle*
- *Gloss varnish*
- *Small dish or saucer, about 4 in (10cm) diameter*
- *Knife*
- *Fine brass beading wire*
- *Medium gauge wire for hanging, about 8 in (20cm) long*
- *Gold paint*

1 To make each stamp, form a ball of clay and press it down onto the tile to make a disc about ⅛ in (3mm) thick. The disc should be a little larger than the coin you want to duplicate. Brush the clay surface with talcum powder and press one side of the coin firmly onto it. Remove carefully. Repeat with a second disc to make a stamp for the other side of the coin, and then make pairs of stamps for each of the remaining coins. Bake the stamps on the tile for 20 minutes.

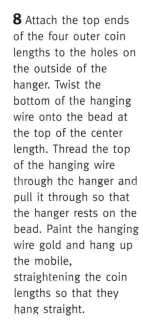

2 To make a polymer clay coin, press a ball of black clay onto a piece of baking parchment to make a disc about the same size as the coin you are duplicating. The baking parchment allows you to peel the clay disc off easily without distorting it.

4 Repeat with different pairs of stamps to make at least 20 coins. Brush both sides of every coin with metallic powders, some gold, some silver, and so on, to make a collection of gleaming coins. Make small holes in the top and bottom of each coin for hanging. Bake all the coins for 20 minutes and varnish.

6 Brush the clay surface with talcum powder and use some of the stamps to stamp around the edge of the hanger. Make a hole in the center of the hanger and four smaller holes evenly spaced round the edge. Make a ¼ in (6mm) bead of gold or black clay. Bake the hanger on the dish, as well as the small bead, for 30 minutes. Ease the hanger off the dish while it is warm.

8 Attach the top ends of the four outer coin lengths to the holes on the outside of the hanger. Twist the bottom of the hanging wire onto the bead at the top of the center length. Thread the top of the hanging wire through the hanger and pull it through so that the hanger rests on the bead. Paint the hanging wire gold and hang up the mobile, straightening the coin lengths so that they hang straight.

3 Lay a stamp on the work surface with the imprinted side upwards and brush with talcum powder. Place the clay disc on this and lay the second stamp, imprinted side down and brushed with talc, on top. Press firmly down, so that the clay disc sandwiched between the two stamps, is impressed on both sides simultaneously.

5 To make the mobile hanger, roll out a sheet of gold clay and lay it over a small dish for a former. Trim the clay neatly all round. As an alternative to gold clay, you could use black clay and brush it with gold powder.

7 Join the coins together with twisted brass beading wire, leaving a gap of about 2 in (50mm) between each pair of coins. You will need four lengths of three or four coins for the outside and one length, for the center, with five coins. Attach the bead to the top of the center length.

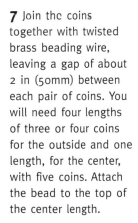

PAINTING

A simple silk cord is all that is needed to turn a painted disc bead into a beautiful pendant.

Baked polymer clay has an excellent surface for painting and this technique will add beautiful effects to polymer clay art, jewelry, miniatures, and sculpture.

Use only acrylic paints for surface painting on polymer clay. Enamel paints or paints thinned with mineral spirits (turpentine substitute) will never dry properly on the clay. It is important to de-grease the surface, or the water-based acrylic paint will bead and refuse to adhere: brush over the surface with alcohol of some kind such as denatured alcohol (methylated spirits).

On some of the clays, the paint may bleed into the surrounding areas after a period of

PAINTING BEADS

Man has been painting beads for centuries and this is an exciting technique that can produce miniature works of art.

1 Push the bead to be painted onto a large darning needle, so that it jams in place and gives you something to hold. Varnish and de-grease the bead. Hold the bead by the darning needle in one hand and rest the needle on the rim of the bowl. Steady your painting hand on the other side of the bowl. You will find you can rotate the bead by turning the needle and so paint concentric lines evenly.

2 For bold hatching effects and stripes on beads, simply steady the bead on the darning needle and paint. Acrylic paint is opaque, so you can paint light onto dark clay for some stunning effects. If you make a mistake, you can simply scrape away the paint and begin again.

YOU WILL NEED

- *Polymer clay beads*
- *Large darning needle*
- *Gloss or matt varnish*
- *Denatured alcohol (methylated spirits)*
- *Small bowl*
- *Acrylic paint*
- *Fine artists' paintbrushes*
- *Water pot*
- *Paper or card for a mixing palette*

3 Chinese brush painting techniques work very well on polymer clay beads, and you can use stone effect clays to provide the perfect background. Here, a bird on a bamboo is painted using single brush strokes for each leaf.

DIP DOT ROSES

1 This is another painting technique that works beautifully on polymer clay beads. The roses are created by dipping a knitting needle into the paint and dotting it onto the beads. First, varnish and de-grease the beads as above. Apply a dot of light pink and a dot of dark red side by side on the bead.

Dip dot roses make stylish jewelry. Here, gilt metal spacers are used to accent the beads.

time, and to avoid this you can first paint on a coat of matt or gloss varnish as a barrier. When the varnish is dry, de-grease the surface and then paint. As a final protection, especially in the case of beads that are to be worn, brush the painted area with another coat of gloss or matt varnish. Miniature china should have a final coat of gloss to make the paint shine like a real glaze.

Always use good quality artists' paintbrushes, which give you a fine point for painting. Brushes with hairs of man-made fibers are best for acrylic paint.

For details of painting faces for sculpture, see page 77.

A miniature tea set with a tiny rose design. The teapot is about ¾ in (19mm) tall.

YOU WILL NEED

- *Polymer clay beads*
- *Gloss or matt varnish*
- *Denatured alcohol (methylated spirits)*
- *Acrylic paint*
- *Water pot*
- *Knitting needle or cocktail stick*

2 Wipe the knitting needle and then use it to swirl the two colors together into a spiral, to suggest a rose. Only do this once; if you are not happy with the result, wipe off the paint and start again.

3 Dip the needle into the dark green paint and mark a series of dots in a spiral from the base of the rose, to make a stem. The dots will become smaller as the paint on the needle is used up. Apply larger dots of dark green on either side of the rose, and on the stem. Use the needle to pull the dots into points to make leaves.

PAINTING MINIATURE CHINA

YOU WILL NEED

- *Polymer clay miniature china*
- *Gloss varnish*
- *Denatured alcohol (methylated spirits)*
- *Acrylic paint*
- *Water pot*
- *Fine paintbrush*

De-grease and varnish the china, as above. Use very fine brushes for painting motifs on miniature china. Spot motifs and natural subjects like these flowers are much easier to paint than concentric lines or repeating patterns. Keep the patterns simple and just paint single strokes and spots for petals and leaves. Apply a coat of gloss varnish when the paint is dry.

IMAGE TRANSFERS

The beige clay background gives the transferred image an antique look. The sails of the original copy were colored white, which gives the transfer pleasing highlights.

Like several other plastic compounds, polymer clay can pick up images from printed paper. The great bonus with polymer clay is that the image can be baked permanently into the clay. The best images to use for this technique are prints from photocopiers and lazer printers that have toner rather than ink. Fresh prints will work

SIMPLE IMAGE TRANSFERS

In this sequence, a lazer copy of a 19th Century ship engraving is colored with colored pencils and transferred to the clay. Images transferred by this technique will be a mirror of the original, so images with lettering are not suitable.

1 Roll out a sheet of clay on the tile and trim to just larger than the image to be transferred. Trim away any excess paper border round the image. Use the colored pencils to color in the image, pressing hard so that the color is strong, as it will pale during the transfer process.

2 Lay the paper, image side down, on the clay and burnish all over the back of the image with the modeling tool. Be sure that the paper is in contact with the clay all over its surface or there will be gaps in the transferred image. Lay a second tile on top of the paper and bake for 20 minutes.

YOU WILL NEED

- *Polymer clay: beige*
- *Two ceramic tiles*
- *Roller*
- *Lazer print or photocopy of a black and white drawing*
- *Colored pencils*
- *Smooth modeling tool for burnishing*

3 When the tiles are cool enough to handle, remove the top tile and peel back the paper. The image and most of the coloring should have transferred to the surface of the clay. You can now use the clay panel for jewelry, as a box lid, or in any other way. Do not sand the image or the transfer will be removed.

ENAMELED IMAGE TRANSFERS

This technique was originally developed by Gwen Gibson to give sumptuous enameled effects. In this example, a Celtic motif is used to give the appearance of an illuminated manuscript. The image is transferred onto the back of a thin sheet of translucent clay through which it is then viewed. The resulting image is therefore not reversed, and the technique can be used for text and calligraphy.

better than older ones. Colored pencils and pastels will also transfer successfully and can be used to color images before transferring. Once baked into the clay, the images can be painted, gilded, varnished, antiqued, or even covered with a layer of translucent clay and baked to provide an embedded image.

This piece uses the enameled image technique with a pencil-colored original, omitting the paint and leaf.

The finished Celtic image is surrounded by a gilded rope of black clay and re-baked. It is then glued to a brooch pin or a hairclip, as above.

YOU WILL NEED

- *Polymer clay: transparent, beige*
- *Two ceramic tiles*
- *Baking parchment*
- *Lazer or photocopy of a Celtic motif*
- *Acrylic paint: red, blue, yellow, green*
- *Brush*
- *Pencil*
- *Scissors*
- *Imitation gold leaf*
- *Craft glue*

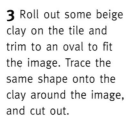

2 Brush the image with denatured alcohol to de-grease and then paint the design with the acrylic paints, applying the paint thickly so that the colors are strong.

3 Roll out some beige clay on the tile and trim to an oval to fit the image. Trace the same shape onto the clay around the image, and cut out.

4 Apply gold leaf to the beige backing clay (see page 90). Spread a thin coat of PVA glue over the leaf and press the transferred image, image side down, onto the glue.

5 Press all over the clay surface to eliminate any air bubbles. The glue will stick the baked clay to the gold leaf. Cover with a tile and bake again for 30 minutes. When the piece is cool, sand and buff the surface so that the image, with its gold leaf backing, shows through clearly. You can now mount the piece in a clay mount to make a brooch or a pendant.

1 Roll out the transparent clay on the baking parchment to prevent sticking. It needs to be about ¹⁄₁₆ in (2mm) thick or less. Make a transfer, as above, using the Celtic motif. Bake, cool, and remove the paper from the baked clay.

ENAMEL EFFECTS

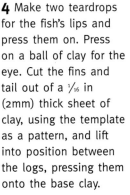

The finished piece shows the lovely, glassy effect produced with cold enamels. The tiny brooch has its background filled with enamel as well.

Cloisonné is a fascinating subject, and soon after discovering polymer clay, I decided it was an ideal medium to simulate this beautiful craft.

While the polymer clay could be used for the metal, I needed something to use for enamel, and the obvious answer was cold (or epoxy) enamels. These are a form of liquid plastic

FISH PLAQUE

YOU WILL NEED

- *Polymer clay: gold*
- *Roller*
- *Ceramic tile*
- *Tracing paper and pencil*
- *Circle cutter 2½ in (65mm) diameter (or use a circle of stiff card of the same measurement and cut round it)*
- *Knife*
- *Darning needle*
- *Brush protector or drinking straw*
- *Cold enamels: transparent red, transparent green, opaque white*
- *Hardener*
- *Plastic mixing cups*
- *Cocktail sticks*
- *Cardboard shoe box or similar*
- *Gold metallic paste*

1 Roll out a sheet of gold clay, ⅛ in (3mm) thick, on the tile and use the cutter to cut out a circle of clay. Trace the template onto tracing paper, lay it onto the clay circle, and draw over the lines of the design with the needle to inscribe them onto the clay.

2 Mark in the fish's scales with the brush protector, holding it at an angle so that the end makes tiny crescents all over the fish's body.

3 Form long logs of gold clay, for the cloisonné wires, about ⅟₃₂ in (1mm) thick. Leave one end of each log thicker for a handle. Use these to outline the design, cutting them to length, and pressing each log down so that it seals along its length onto the base clay.

4 Make two teardrops for the fish's lips and press them on. Press on a ball of clay for the eye. Cut the fins and tail out of a ⅟₁₆ in (2mm) thick sheet of clay, using the template as a pattern, and lift into position between the logs, pressing them onto the base clay.

TEMPLATE
The template is reproduced actual size so can be traced directly off the page.

which, when mixed with a hardener, harden into a permanent, glassy material almost identical to true enamel. Experiment showed that cold enamels were compatible and durable when used on polymer clay, so the following technique was born.

Transparent liquid polymer clay can be used instead of cold enamels but it is not as transparent and needs sanding and buffing to make it shine.

Polymer clay cloisonné can be made into beautiful pendants and brooches. You could also brush metallic powder over the piece before baking, but varnish before applying enamel.

VARIATIONS

- *The main pictures show more examples of polymer clay cloisonné. Some of the pieces have had their cells (areas for the enamel) deepened to enhance the effect*
- *Combinations of opaque and transparent enamel give even more variety*

5 Texture the fins and tail with a needle or modeling tool, and pierce a hole in the center of the eye. Check that all the wires are pressed down firmly and that the joins where they meet, or butt against each other, do not have any gaps. Texture the background with the cut end of a cocktail stick to suggest some bubbles.

6 If you wish, make a twisted strip to surround the whole piece. Bake the piece on the tile for 30 minutes and cool on the tile. Mix the transparent red enamel with the hardener in the proportions given on the bottle (usually 1:1 or 2:1). Stir thoroughly to mix and leave to stand for ten minutes so that any bubbles dissipate.

7 Using the cocktail stick, scoop up some of the enamel and drop it onto the center of the fish's body, pushing it into the corners with the point of the stick. Work your way along the fish, adding more drops of enamel as necessary, and spreading them with the cocktail stick until the whole area is filled to a depth just below the top of the logs.

8 Repeat with the transparent green enamel for the weeds and the white enamel for the fish's head. Cover the piece with a cardboard box to protect it from dust and leave to set for 24 hours. The enamel will become hard and have a glassy surface. Use the metallic paste to highlight the bare surface of the gold clay.

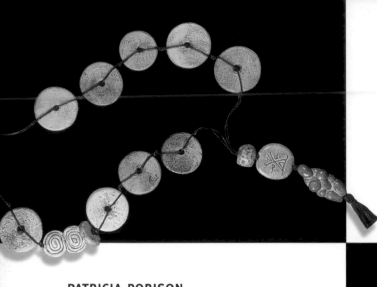

SUE HEASER
CELTIC CROSS JEWELLERY
This sumptuous simulated
Victorian silver jewelry is based on
the Celtic Cross symbol. Faux
polymer clay turquoises
and agates are
mounted in
simulated
filigree silver.

PATRICIA ROBISON
VENUS NECKLACE
This wonderful necklace with the patina
of ages uses several techniques, including
texturing, and antiquing with paint and
soft clay. The tiny sculpted statuette is
based on a prehistoric figure.

HEN SCOTT
BOWL OF EGGS
A faux verdigris polymer clay bowl with
tripod legs cups a trio of mokumé gané
bantam's eggs. The elegant design
combines with the contrasting textures
to produce an outstanding objet d'art

KAREN LEWIS
DRUM BEADS
Faux ivory and jade beads
in luscious muted colors
are applied with tiny cane
slices to make these
fabulous beads.

GWEN GIBSON
ENAMELED MINIATURE
Gwen Gibson has developed this gorgeous technique of simulating antique artwork. She uses photo transfer, paint, and gold leaf.

CHRISTINE ALIBERT
MOKUMÉ GANÉ EARRINGS
Colored clays are layered with translucent clay and silver leaf for these dazzling earrings. The simple circle design shows off the technique to perfection.

JODY BISHEL
PRIMITIVE PINS
A backfill of liquid polymer clay has been used to decorate and age these unique pins. Human hair and metal wire complete the design.

CLAY SIMULATIONS & INCLUSIONS

Polymer clay is a wonderful medium for simulating virtually any material. The techniques involved are as diverse as the exciting results.

DONA KATO
VERDIGRIS VESSELS
These two beautifully crafted vessels are made from translucent clay with green embossing powder inclusions. A small, sculpted bird adds a delightful finishing touch to one of the vessels, while faux bone and metal complete the other.

BASIC
INCLUSIONS
TECHNIQUES

The green pendant contains embossing powder; the blue one includes red and blue art sand.

Polymer clay can be mixed with a wide variety of materials to texture and embellish the clay. This can range from black sand mixed into translucent clay, which simulates granite, to nutmeg mixed into dark brown clay for a miniature chocolate cake.

The main rule when choosing material to mix into polymer clay is that it should be an inert and bone-dry substance. Anything that could rot or react with the clay should be avoided. You can mix inclusions into any color clay; opaque clay with inclusions will give a textured surface; using translucent clay will reveal the inclusions below the surface, particularly if the clay is sanded and buffed.

BASIC METHOD
Adding inclusions is a simple process and virtually the same for all ingredients.

YOU WILL NEED

- Polymer clay
- Material for including
- Saucer or small bowl
- For firmer clays: mixing or softening agent

1 Pour the material you want to mix with the clay into a saucer. Here, ground nutmeg is to be mixed into translucent clay. Flatten the clay into a pancake and press it onto the nutmeg. Fold it in half and roll and fold as though you were marbling the clay (see page 17).

2 Flatten the clay again and repeat the process until the material is evenly spread throughout the clay. You may need to cut opaque clay in half to check. If the mixture is very stiff or becomes dry as you mix, you can add a mixing agent or clay diluent to soften it. Finally, form the clay into a cabochon, or use as required.

3 These cabochons show translucent clay mixed, from top to bottom, with: blue and red art sand; verdigris embossing powder; dried oregano; nutmeg.

Sanding and buffing has made the faux pebbles in this necklace shine.

SAFE INCLUSION MATERIALS

Sand You can use ordinary beach or silver sand, or one of the colored sands sold for sand art.

Embossing powders Available in many different colors and color combinations.

Dried herbs Herbs such as oregano, basil, and parsley give a lovely internal flecking to translucent clay and can simulate moss agate.

Seeds and grains These are particularly useful for miniatures: semolina mixed into beige clays makes beautiful crumbly miniature bread, while poppy seeds suggest miniature currants.

Fibers and threads Short lengths of colored fiber and silk look gorgeous in sheets of translucent clay.

Polymer clay Baked clay pieces used as inclusions will cause a textured surface that can be left as it is, or sanded smooth. Unbaked clay gives more subtle effects that are excellent when used for semi-precious stone simulations.

GRATING POLYMER CLAY

In order to simulate the chaotic nature of natural stones such as quartz, lapis lazuli, or humble beach pebbles, I have found that an ordinary kitchen grater is an invaluable tool. The grated clay gives completely random sized pieces that can then be clumped together to make various matrices. Varying the coarseness of the grater adds even more variety. This technique can also be used in miniatures to produce effects such as fruit cake and sausage meat.

YOU WILL NEED

- *Grater with large and small grating holes*
- *Polymer clay in the colors required—here translucent, white, and black*
- *Quilt batting (wadding) for adding surface texture*

1 It is easiest to grate clay when it is cool and firm so either grate directly from the block or chill any mixed clay in the refrigerator. The softer the clay, the larger the grated particles will be. Using the large holes of the grater, grate some white and translucent clay. Press both colored gratings together into a rough ball and grate again to make the flecks smaller.

2 Using the smaller holes of the grater, grate some black clay. The brand used here is a firm clay, so the particles are very small.

3 Press all the gratings together into a ball and then roll gently in your hands to form into a pebble or cabochon. At this point the clay can be pressed into a mold (see Jade on page 108) to simulate carved stone or made into beads.

4 This shows a range of sample polymer clay pebbles made using this technique, with the black and white pebble, demonstrated here in my hand. The blue-gray bead pebble on the quilt batting has been pressed all over in the batting to give it a sandstone texture. The shiny pebble has been sanded and buffed.

SEMI-PRECIOUS STONES

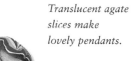

Translucent agate slices make lovely pendants.

Simulating semi-precious stones with polymer clay is an exciting series of techniques that produces quite remarkable results. The translucent clays, in particular, are perfect ingredients for a wide variety of recipes that produce look-alikes which are hard to distinguish from the genuine article. All simulated polymer clay stones should be sanded and buffed for the best effect.

There are many different methods of simulating semi-precious stones and they are as diverse as the stones that they simulate. The following techniques have been developed over years of working both with ancient jewelry and polymer clay—I hope you will find them rewarding.

SIMULATIONS AND INCLUSIONS

AGATE

Recipes

All the recipes in the semi-precious stones simulation techniques use Premo Sculpey polymer clay. If you use a different brand, you will need to choose colors as close as possible to those shown in the photographs.

YOU WILL NEED	MIXTURE
• Polymer clay: white, translucent, copper, ecru • Roller or pasta machine • Table knife • Sharp blade	• Translucent copper = 4 parts translucent + 1 part copper

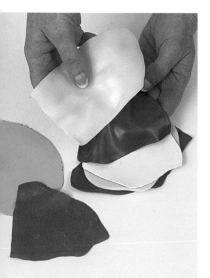

1 Roll out sheets of the different colored clays, varying the thickness of the sheets between $\frac{1}{32}$ in (1mm) and $\frac{1}{8}$ in (3mm). You can have several sheets of some or all of the colors if you wish. Cut each sheet into a rough circle. Pile the sheets, one on top of the other, starting with a white sheet, ending with a copper sheet, and alternating the different colors.

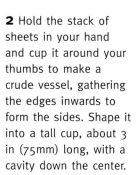

2 Hold the stack of sheets in your hand and cup it around your thumbs to make a crude vessel, gathering the edges inwards to form the sides. Shape it into a tall cup, about 3 in (75mm) long, with a cavity down the center.

3 Form a $\frac{1}{2}$ in (13mm) thick log of translucent clay, 3 in (75mm) long, and insert it into the hollow. Press the colored sheets firmly onto the log to eliminate air spaces.

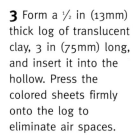

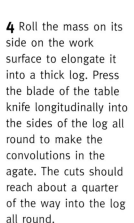

4 Roll the mass on its side on the work surface to elongate it into a thick log. Press the blade of the table knife longitudinally into the sides of the log all round to make the convolutions in the agate. The cuts should reach about a quarter of the way into the log all round.

AGATE

Agates are one of the most popular semi-precious stones and they occur naturally in an enormous range of colors and patterns. When cut open, a common agate has a distinct rough outer skin and concentric, sometimes convoluted, bands of alternating opaque and translucent colors inside. They can be virtually any color but earth colors are most common. The recipe below is for a reddish-brown agate but you can adapt it to make any color.

ONYX

Onyx is a similar stone to agate but it has straight rather than curved bands. It is usually found in stripes of black, white, and brown. I have added gold polymer clay to my mixture to add a sparkle.

Onyx makes sophisticated jewelry. The drop earrings are blocks of onyx, cut to shape and with their edges chamfered.

5 Roll the log on its side to reduce it to the size of cross section you want. This will also reduce the bands inside to make them more detailed. Cut the rounded end off the log and then cut slices as required to apply over a cabochon or make into jewelry. The photograph also shows blue agates, one with a banded center made from layered white and translucent clay.

ONYX

YOU WILL NEED

- *Polymer clay: black, raw sienna, translucent, white, gold*
- *Roller*
- *Blade*

MIXTURES

- *Translucent brown = 1 raw sienna + 2 translucent*
- *Translucent white = 1 white + 1 translucent*

1 Roll out sheets of the black, translucent brown, translucent, translucent white, and gold clays. Make the brown, black, and gold sheets between $1/16$ in (2mm) and $1/4$ in (6mm) thick, and the rest between $1/32$ (1mm) and $1/16$ in (2mm) thick. Stack the sheets up into a loaf consisting of random layers.

2 Roll the top of the loaf to compress the layers and cut thin slices. The resulting sheets can be used to cover cabochons or to wrap around beads.

TURQUOISE

Turquoise is a beautiful stone that has been mined for over 3,000 years. It is prized for its glorious color, which varies from pale blue to green depending on the origin of the stone. Sky blue turquoise from Persia is often the most prized and that is what this recipe has been modeled on. The resulting mixture can be left plain, or traced with a wonderful spider's web pattern, as in the following step-by-step sequence.

This polymer clay link bracelet is inspired by an ancient Egyptian bracelet. Black logs, stamped and silvered, surround each stone, and the pieces are linked with silver jump rings.

TURQUOISE

YOU WILL NEED

- *Polymer clay: turquoise, ultramarine blue, cobalt blue, white, translucent, gold*
- *Grater*
- *Acrylic paint: burnt umber, black*
- *Paintbrush*
- *Small pot*
- *Blade*

MIXTURES

- *Turquoise base = 2 parts turquoise + 1 part white + 1 part ultramarine*

- *Pale turquoise = 1 part turquoise + 1 part cobalt blue + 3 parts white*

1 Mix up the pale turquoise (shown in the cube here) and place in the freezer to harden. Mix the turquoise base and place in the refrigerator to cool. This will make both colors easier to grate, and harden the pale turquoise so that it can be grated finely.

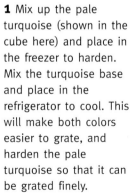

2 Grate the turquoise base using the large holes on the grater. Form the resulting gratings into rough balls of many sizes. Do not press too hard, and leave some of them as half open curls.

3 Put some burnt umber acrylic paint into a small pot and add a little black paint. Mix lightly so that the paint is streaky. Place the turquoise pieces into the pot and stir them round with the brush until they are fully covered with paint. Tip them out onto a sheet of paper and spread apart to dry.

This engraved and inlaid cabochon, right, was inscribed while the clay was soft and then baked. Gold metallic paste was rubbed into the recessed area, excess paste wiped off, and the piece polished. This type of ornament is typical of those found in ancient Persia.

Cabouchons and beads display the intricate random traceries of this technique. Try varying the colors of your mixtures for different shades of turquoise.

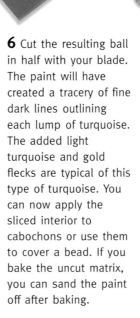

4 Using the small holes of the grater, grate some of the chilled pale turquoise mixture into tiny particles. Grate a tiny quantity of gold clay directly from the block to make tiny flecks of gold.

5 Stir the turquoise base pieces, now coated with dry paint, and the pale turquoise and gold particles together, then press them into a ball. You need to avoid air spaces in the clump but do not press too hard or you will distort the matrix within.

6 Cut the resulting ball in half with your blade. The paint will have created a tracery of fine dark lines outlining each lump of turquoise. The added light turquoise and gold flecks are typical of this type of turquoise. You can now apply the sliced interior to cabochons or use them to cover a bead. If you bake the uncut matrix, you can sand the paint off after baking.

JADE

Jade has been carved by the Chinese for over 2,000 years and used as a decorative stone by many cultures, from the Indians of Central America to the Maoris of New Zealand. It comes in many shades of green, depending on whether it is nephrite jade or jadeite. The latter can also be pink, lilac, orange, or black.

Jade made from polymer clay is remarkably realistic and, with the use of push molds, even carved jade ornaments can be made with ease. The color simulated here is nephrite jade, which is the more common color of stone.

Use simulated jade in push molds for pendants and buttons. Jade beads can be carved and filed for authentic effects.

SIMULATIONS AND INCLUSIONS

JADE

YOU WILL NEED

- Polymer clay: translucent, green, burnt umber, black
- Grater
- Push molds
- Talcum powder
- Paintbrush

MIXTURE

- Dark green = 2 parts green + 1 part burnt umber

- Jade mix = 1 part dark green + 16 parts translucent: mix until streaky

1 Grate the streaky jade mix through the large holes on the grater. Pack the clay together and grate for a finer speckle.

2 Grate the black clay straight from the block through the small holes on the grater. Flatten the grated jade clay mix into a pancake and apply a scant sprinkle of the black flecks to both sides. Roll up and press together so that there are flecks inside the clay and some on the surface.

3 To make 'carved' jade, use a push mold with floral or animal forms, such as this one taken from a flower button. Brush the inside of the mold with talcum powder and press the jade mix firmly into the mold. Ease the clay out of the mold and bake. When cool, buff to a shine.

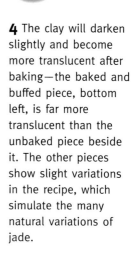

4 The clay will darken slightly and become more translucent after baking—the baked and buffed piece, bottom left, is far more translucent than the unbaked piece beside it. The other pieces show slight variations in the recipe, which simulate the many natural variations of jade.

ROSE QUARTZ

This is a pretty stone that looks particularly good combined with pearls and silver beads. Here it is used to make disc beads.

This necklace is made with simulated rose quartz beads combined with purchased pearl and silver beads. It would make a lovely gift for a bridesmaid.

ROSE QUARTZ

YOU WILL NEED

- *Polymer clay: translucent, alizarin crimson*
- *Grater*
- *Brush protector or drinking straw*

1 Alizarin crimson is a very concentrated color and this photograph shows that only a tiny quantity is needed to color the large ball of translucent clay. Mix this tiny trace into the translucent clay until it is streaky, like the pale log. Mix a trace more alizarin crimson into half of the pale log to make a slightly stronger pink, as can be seen in the second log.

2 Press the two logs together and grate coarsely. At this point, the light parts of the clay look whiter than they will once the clay is baked. The baked cabochon and disc bead in the photograph show how the color changes subtly.

3 Clump the gratings together and form them Into a ball. Press this down onto the work surface to flatten it into a circular disc. Cut a hole out of the center with the brush protector and smooth the cut edges. Bake and buff to a shine (see page 23).

LAPIS LAZULI

The intense blue of lapis lazuli is legendary and this stone has been used for jewelry since prehistoric times. It is reputed to protect the wearer from evil. The color can vary depending on the origin of the stone but it is usually a deep blue with flecks of white calcite and sparkles of pyrite. The simulated polymer clay version is remarkably realistic.

A lapis lazuli cabochon makes a superb pendant mounted in a polymer clay setting. Metallic powder is used for the gold.

AMBER, IVORY, AND BONE

Amber combines perfectly with silver polymer clay and black glass beads.

LAPIS LAZULI

YOU WILL NEED

- *Polymer clay: ultramarine blue, translucent*
- *Imitation gold leaf*
- *Grater*

1 Grate the ultramarine and translucent clays straight from the block using the fine holes on the grater. You will only need a small quantity of the translucent to provide a few calcite flecks. Press a scrap of gold leaf on the block of ultramarine clay and grate to make a sprinkle of gold.

2 Press together all the grated pieces and form into beads or cabochons. Do not try to mix the clay too much or the colors will become streaky. After baking, the clay will darken considerably into a rich lapis blue, as shown by the left-hand pieces in the photograph.

AMBER

YOU WILL NEED

- *Polymer clay: translucent, zinc yellow, alizarin crimson*

MIXTURES

- *Orange amber = 1 part zinc yellow + 16 parts translucent + trace alizarin crimson*

- *Yellow amber = 1 part zinc yellow + 16 parts translucent + 3 parts orange amber*

1 Use the above recipes to make a streaky log of each color. Be extremely sparing with the alizarin crimson, because it is a saturated color. Press the two logs together and marble a few times so that there are distinct streaks of the two colors still visible.

Amber is a magical substance. It is the fossilized resin from pine trees that grew in primeval forests and its glorious golden color has attracted man since the earliest times. It is not possible to simulate the beautiful clear amber in polymer clay but cloudy amber is easily mimicked. As with all semi-precious stones, the color of amber varies considerably from pale honey to dark gold, so slight variations in your mixtures will only serve to make your faux amber more realistic.

With the vital restrictions on the sale of ivory in place to protect endangered species, simulated ivory is now the only environmentally acceptable kind. Polymer clay ivory and bone are easy to make and can be decorated by molding, carving, and inscribing in much the same way as the real materials. The simple marbling technique given here works well for both bone and ivory. To make ivory, just marble the colors further to give a smoother result.

Simulated bone and ivory looks very effective when molded, as here. You can also use it in sheets to make boxes.

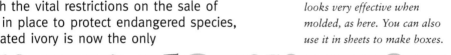

2 Cut the streaked log into lengths and shape into beads. Try to retain the streaks all aligned along the bead and allow any fold in the clay to remain for further realism. The disc bead shown is modeled on a Roman bead, while cylinder and bicone beads are all typical of amber craftsmanship. You can also grate the amber colors for a more mottled amber. Sand and polish the beads for an authentic shine.

BONE AND IVORY

YOU WILL NEED

- *Polymer clay: translucent, white, ecru*
- *Push molds for carved bone or ivory effects*

MIXTURE

- *Translucent white = 2 parts translucent + 1 part white*

1 Form a thick log of translucent white mix and a thin log each of translucent and ecru clays. Press together and marble until the streaks are fine but still visible (see page 17). For ivory, continue marbling until the streaks are very fine indeed or barely visible.

2 Cut lengths of the marbled mixture as required. Be sure to keep the lines of marbling oriented in one direction and avoid any loops or swirls developing. You have to think that you are simulating a piece that has been carved out a hard substance with all streaks lying in the same direction. The finished molded piece shown here has been antiqued with acrylic paint (see page 114).

MOKUMÉ GANÉ

This technique, which is pronounced 'mok-u-may gan-ay', is a traditional Japanese metal working skill that can be recreated in polymer clay with spectacular results. Nan Roche, in The New Clay, first pointed out that mokumé gané was adaptable to polymer clay work and many people have since enjoyed and developed this simple and extremely beautiful technique.

The original method involves stacking layers of different metals, rolling them thin, punching the surface and then slicing it off to reveal an effect that suggests metallic wood grain. The polymer clay version can involve different colored clays, or a combination of colors, translucent clay, and metal leafs.

These exquisite mokumé gané drop earrings show off the luxurious, highly decorative effects of this specialist technique.

SIMULATIONS AND INCLUSIONS

MOKUMÉ GANÉ BLOCKS

YOU WILL NEED

- *Polymer clay: background color, translucent*
- *Baking parchment*
- *Roller or pasta machine*
- *Imitation gold leaf*
- *Soft paintbrush*
- *Wide soft paintbrush*
- *Blunt tool*
- *Sharp blade*

1 Roll out the translucent clay as thinly as possible. This is easier if you roll the clay between two sheets of baking parchment. If you use a pasta machine, pass the clay through, sandwiched between parchment sheets.

2 Cut a square sheet of clay, about 4 in (100mm) square and lay it on the parchment. Apply a sheet of imitation gold leaf to the clay, carefully holding the leaf by the edges and using a brush to help you.

3 Use a wide, soft paintbrush to brush down the leaf onto the clay surface. Trim away any excess leaf around the edge to use in the next layer of leaf.

4 Cut another sheet of translucent clay and press it onto the sheet of leaf. Roll the surface very lightly to eliminate air bubbles but do not press too hard or the leaf will fracture. Continue building up alternating layers of thin clay sheet and leaf. You can use scraps of leaf to fill in any spaces in the layers.

5 When you have built up about five double layers, finish with a layer of clay, and cut the block in half. Apply a sheet of leaf to the top of one half and stack the other on top so that you have about 11 layers of leaf in the sandwich.

The method given here uses uncolored translucent clay and imitation gold leaf, which is then sliced and applied to a background of colored clay. I find that this gives me a mokumé gané slicing block that is extremely versatile and can be used for many different colored projects by varying the background color. You could also vary the color of the leaf, or tint the translucent clay as you wish.

Use translucent clay with the highest translucency possible for the best effect. Sanding and buffing baked mokumé gané is important in order to achieve high translucency to reveal the different layers beneath the surface.

The slices cut from a mokumé gané block can be used to decorate sheets of clay for jewelry and boxes. It can also be applied to the surface of beads or used to cover vessels and frames.

The colored clay backing shows through the layers of gold and translucent mokumé gané.

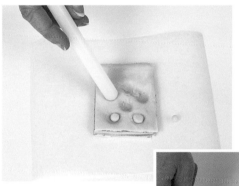

6 Press deep dents into the block with a blunt tool. You can make these regular or random, depending on the final effect you want. Do not press right through to the bottom. Form small balls and ovals of translucent clay and press these into the dents so that they are filled with clay.

7 Turn the block over and press over it with your fingers so that you can feel where the clay balls were applied on the underside. Depress the clay around these areas so that you have a series of hillocks in the clay surface.

8 Use your blade to shave off the top of the hillocks and set these pieces aside for using as infill later. Now take further horizontal slices, about $\frac{1}{32}$ in (1mm) thick, from the raised areas. With each slice, you will find that the leaf will be revealed in concentric but irregular rings, rather like wood grain or shot silk. These slices are now used to decorate sheets of clay.

9 To make a panel or box lid, roll out a sheet of blue clay, $\frac{1}{8}$ in (3mm) thick, and trim to the size required. Cut slices from the mokumé gané block and lay them on the blue sheet. Fill in any gaps with the earlier smaller slices or translucent clay. Roll over the surface lightly to smooth it. Bake and, when cool, sand and buff the piece to a high shine to reveal the translucence.

ANTIQUING EFFECTS

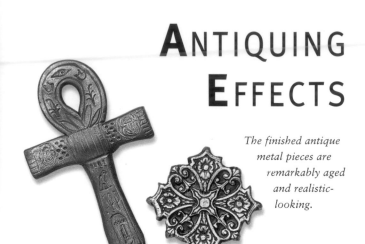

The finished antique metal pieces are remarkably aged and realistic-looking.

The old and the antique have never been more popular than they are today. Home decorating books are filled with advice on distressing, ageing, and antiquing, while shops are bursting with replicas of ancient artifacts. If you enjoy antiquity and the art of long ago, you will find great delight in simulating the patina of ages past onto your polymer clay creations.

Both jewelry and miniatures can benefit from these techniques. Simulated metal polymer clay beads take on a wonderful authenticity if they are slightly tarnished, while a dollhouse kitchen will look far more realistic with worn or used kitchen utensils.

ANTIQUING METAL

Most metals will corrode, tarnish, or discolor in time and even those that do not will collect the grime of ages in recessed areas. Bronze artefacts from archeological sites attain a wonderful patina of verdigris, and the first method given here demonstrates how to simulate this with a verdigris ankh, an ancient Egyptian amulet.

YOU WILL NEED

- *Polymer clay: dark turquoise green, dark brown*
- *Ceramic tile*
- *Small roller*
- *Blunt tapestry needle*
- *Bronze metallic paste*

MIXTURE

Verdigris = 2 parts turquoise + 1 part dark brown

1 Form the verdigris mixture into a ³⁄₈ in (10mm) thick log. Cut lengths of this to assemble into a T-shape on the tile. Form a loop above the T, to make the ankh shape. Roll over the clay to flatten it and compress the pieces together.

2 Decorate the ankh with inscribed lines using the tapestry needle. Egyptian hieroglyphs are beautiful motifs to copy and you can add hatching, dots, and lines, as you wish. Bake the ankh on the tile for about 30 minutes and allow to cool.

3 Rub bronze metallic paste over the ankh surface with your finger. This will highlight the raised areas and bring out the inscribed design. It also suggests an antique bronze artifact that has worn down to the bright metal under the verdigris. A simple cord tied to the loop of the ankh will make this an attractive pendant.

4 To simulate most other metals, such as silver and polished brass, first make the item using black clay. You can then rub on metallic powders or pastes leaving black clay clearly visible in any recesses. Here, brass metallic paste is rubbed on to molded and baked black clay to simulate an ancient piece of polished brass. The silver pendant used as the original shows how black tarnish collects in recesses.

ANTIQUING BONE AND IVORY

Most carved bone and ivory becomes discolored in time, with the original color showing in the raised areas, where the artifact has been polished by handling, and darkening in the carved niches and incised lines. This is simple to simulate with polymer clay and here, acrylic paint and a 'bone' polymer clay flute are used as an example.

The simple lines of the carving enhance the flute's smooth surface. They are emphasized by the antiquing technique.

BONE FLUTE

To make the flute, cover the handle of a wooden spoon with foil to ensure easy release after baking. Make a bone mixture of clay (see page 111) and then wrap the handle with the clay. Cut holes for the mouth hole and finger holes using a brush protector. Bake the flute on the handle and remove when cool. Plug the mouth hole end of the flute with clay and then bake again. You can play this flute by blowing across the mouth hole and it produces a creditable scale! Now carve the flute with a vine, as shown, or with motifs of your choice. For instructions on carving polymer clay, see page 22.

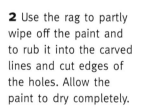

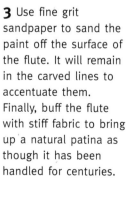

YOU WILL NEED

- *Baked and carved polymer clay simulated bone flute*
- *Denatured alcohol (methylated spirits)*
- *Acrylic paint: burnt umber*
- *Paintbrush*
- *Rag*
- *Sandpaper*
- *Stiff fabric for buffing*

1 Brush over the flute with denatured alcohol to de-grease the surface. Squeeze some burnt umber acrylic paint onto a piece of scrap paper and add a little water so that it flows easily. Brush paint all over the flute with the paintbrush, working it into the carved lines.

2 Use the rag to partly wipe off the paint and to rub it into the carved lines and cut edges of the holes. Allow the paint to dry completely.

3 Use fine grit sandpaper to sand the paint off the surface of the flute. It will remain in the carved lines to accentuate them. Finally, buff the flute with stiff fabric to bring up a natural patina as though it has been handled for centuries.

See also

●

SIMULATIONS
PAGE 104-107
ANTIQUE EFFECTS
PAGES 114-115

Simulating Antique Jewelry

The various simulation

techniques given in this book

give you a rich repertoire from

which to create 'antique' jewelry

of many different kinds.

VICTORIAN PENDANT

This project shows you how to combine techniques to make a simulated Victorian silver jewelry pendant in the shape of a Celtic cross, complete with mounted 'turquoise' and 'agate' stones.

The cross is 1¾ in (45mm) across so you will need to work small and with delicacy to accurately simulate this type of jewelry, which includes silver filigree effects.

YOU WILL NEED

- *Polymer clay: black*
- *Ceramic tile*
- *Knife*
- *Tapestry needle*
- *Polymer clay simulated stones: one ½ in (13mm) round turquoise cabochon; four ¼ in (6mm) round agate cabochons*
- *Silver metallic powder*
- *Paintbrush*
- *Silver-plated pendant mount*
- *Craft glue*
- *Gloss varnish*
- *Silver chain*

VARIATIONS

- *Try making the same design using lapis lazuli and amber stones with gold powders*
- *Cold enamels could be used instead of the faux stones. Make the mounts empty, bake the pendant, and then fill them with the enamel*

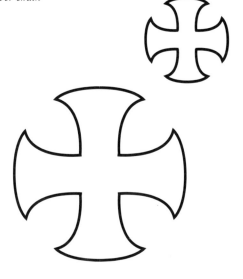

TEMPLATE
This template is shown actual size. Trace and cut out the template as a guide to the pendant shape.

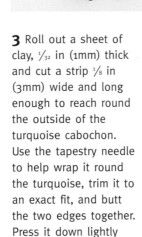

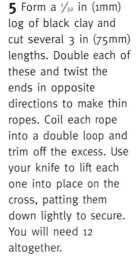

1 Form a 1 in (25mm) ball of the black clay and press it down onto the tile, flattening it into a round disc 3/16 in (5mm) thick and 13/4 in (45mm) in diameter. Trace the template and place it over the disc. Draw along the lines of the template with the needle to make an impression on the clay. Cut out the shape of the cross with your knife held as vertically as possible.

3 Roll out a sheet of clay, 1/32 in (1mm) thick and cut a strip 1/8 in (3mm) wide and long enough to reach round the outside of the turquoise cabochon. Use the tapestry needle to help wrap it round the turquoise, trim it to an exact fit, and butt the two edges together. Press it down lightly onto the cross.

5 Form a 1/32 in (1mm) log of black clay and cut several 3 in (75mm) lengths. Double each of these and twist the ends in opposite directions to make thin ropes. Coil each rope into a double loop and trim off the excess. Use your knife to lift each one into place on the cross, patting them down lightly to secure. You will need 12 altogether.

7 When the pendant is cool, roll out a strip of black clay, 1/2 in (13mm) by 3/8 in (10mm). Apply craft glue to the back of one of the cross arms and press the clay strip on firmly, over the base wire of the pendant mount. The loop of the mount should be just above the top of the cross. Bake again for 20 minutes. When cool, varnish the pendant. The earrings are made in the same way, using smaller stones, and have stud earring pads glued to the backs.

2 Trim away any rough edges with your knife and smooth the sides of the cross with the side of the tapestry needle. Press the baked cabochons into position on the cross

4 To make the agate mounts, roll another sheet of black clay, about 1/32 in (1mm) thick, and cut four 1/32 in (1mm) wide strips. Twist the ends of each one in opposite directions to make a thin twisted rope, and again use the tapestry needle to help push the rope into a ring around each agate. Trim the ends of each and pat down lightly.

6 Brush over the pendant with silver powder but do not let the powder get deep into the crevices, which should remain black for an antique effect. Bake the pendant on the tile for 20-30 minutes.

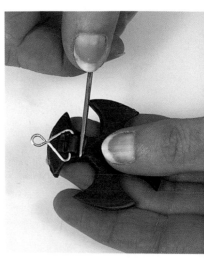

COMBINING TECHNIQUES

MINIATURE CERAMICS

Polymer clay simulates miniature ceramics and pottery even better than the real material! This is because polymer clay has a much finer texture than most ceramic materials, such as stoneware and earthenware clays, and therefore looks more true to scale when made into miniature pieces.

Combined with this, there are many techniques for creating miniature vessels with polymer clay such as balloon vessels (page 67), potting (page 66), and the vase method given here. Handles and lids can be added in the same way as in real pottery techniques.

Simulating the color and texture of miniature ceramics is fun to do and several

Glazes finish off miniature ceramics beautifully. The terracotta base has a brown acrylic paint glaze that has been varnished.

SIMULATIONS AND INCLUSIONS

RECIPES FOR POTTERY TYPES

- *Terracotta = 2 parts mid-brown + 1 part red + white (optional for lightening)*
- *Cream ware = 1 part beige + 1 part white*
- *Cream stoneware = beige with tea bag dust mixed in*
- *Gray stoneware = white + trace of black + trace of blue + tea bag dust*
- *Porcelain = 1 part white + 1 part translucent*

1 This is the mix used for terracotta pots. The vessel in the photograph is about 1 in (25mm) high and has been potted (see page 66). You can give miniature pots a rim by slipping them onto a large paintbrush handle to support the interior and then pressing the handle of a thin paintbrush horizontally against the pot just below the top edge. Work all round the pot, keeping the indentation as even as possible.

2 Tea bag dust is mixed into the clay in the same way as any inclusions. Pour some of the dust into a shallow dish, knead the clay until soft, and then press a flattened pancake onto the dust. Fold in and repeat until the clay is evenly speckled throughout. The cream stoneware vase shown above has tea bag dust inclusions and a yellow glaze.

MINIATURE JUGS AND VESSELS

To make miniature vessels with narrow necks, such as jugs and vases, a different technique to potting is used.

YOU WILL NEED

- *Polymer clay: cream stoneware mix*
- *Blunt tapestry needle*

1 Form a ³⁄₄ in (19mm) ball of clay and shape it into a teardrop. Make a hole about ¹⁄₂ in (13mm) deep in the top with a blunt needle.

recipes are given here. Inclusions will add texture to make speckles in the ceramic body. One of my favorites for miniature ceramics is the dark dust that collects in the bottom of a box of tea bags.

GLAZES

There are a number of ways of making successful glazes for baked miniature pottery. You can use acrylic paint and then gloss varnish painted over it for a shiny glaze. The powder from artists' pastels can be mixed with artists' acrylic medium to give a wonderful variety of transparent glaze colors. Remember to de-grease the baked clay before glazing with acrylic glazes

(see page 94). Liquid polymer clay can also be used to glaze vessels.

GLAZE RECIPES

Using gloss or matt acrylic medium

Honey glaze on terracotta = acrylic medium + burnt sienna artists' pastel

Yellow glaze on cream ware = acrylic medium + yellow ocher artists' pastel

Dark blue on gray stoneware = acrylic medium + Payne's gray (dark blue-gray) artists' paste

2 With the needle held in one hand and the pot supported by the other, make circular movements with the needle. The action is as though you were stirring, but with the tip remaining in the same position. This will flare out the rim of the vase.

3 Roll the neck of the vase between your forefingers to thin it and to smooth the vase into a pleasing shape. You can alter the shape of the vase by thinning the lower part of it at this point.

4 Finally, rotate your fingertip in the top of the vase to open it out further and smooth the rim. Pierce down into the center of the vase again with your needle to give an impression of depth. These miniature vases look perfect when filled with miniature flowers.

5 The basic vase shape can be turned into a jug by the simple addition of a lip. Support the rim of the vase with your thumb and forefinger and pull out a lip with the tip of the tapestry needle.

6 Add a handle to your jug, but be sure that it is exactly opposite the lip. See page 67 for instructions on making a handle.

Stylishly mimicking their full-size counterparts, miniature jugs are easy to make with a little practice.

WOOD

Simulating wood in miniature with polymer clay is as successful as simulating miniature ceramics. The fine grain of the clay and its ability to be marbled means that you can produce a fine wood grain that fits a miniature scale better than most real wood. The wide range of colors combined with color mixing means that virtually every color wood can be mimicked.

Once you have created your wood mixture, there are many techniques you can use to

Miniature furniture made with simulated wood grain clay is remarkably realistic and robust.

SIMULATIONS AND INCLUSIONS

WOODEN VENEERS

YOU WILL NEED

- *Polymer clay: wood grain mixture as above*
- *Roller*

1 Make logs of the different colored clays, all about the same length. The colors shown here are for mixing pine.

2 Press the logs together to make one thick log, keeping all the colors visible on the outside. Roll the log thinner and then fold in half. Do not twist the log but keep all the streaks parallel.

3 Roll the log thin again, fold in half, and continue so that the streaks get thinner and thinner with every fold and roll. You can fold any unattractive areas to the inside as you work. Continue until the streaks are very fine but still distinct. When the clay is rolled into a sheet, the streaks will widen so you need to allow for this.

4 Fold the log in half for the last time and roll flat on your work surface. A typical loop in the grain will occur where the log was folded. The right-hand sheet shows the pine wood grain, the left-hand sheet shows mahogany with gold added, giving a wonderful gleam to the wood effect. The sheets can now be cut up to use as you wish.

turn it into wooden artefacts. The clay can be rolled out and turned into boxes and miniature furniture (see page 68 for instructions on making boxes from sheets). Grooving is demonstrated below and simulates turned miniature wood. You can carve the 'wood' to make beautiful beads and jewelry or mold it to simulate carved items.

Here are some recipes for different woods. All of these can be used in the techniques given below.

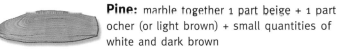

Pine: marble together 1 part beige + 1 part ocher (or light brown) + small quantities of white and dark brown

Mahogany: first make a red brown = 1 part dark brown + 1 part crimson. Marble together 2 parts red brown + 1 part black + 1 part gold

Teak: marble together 1 part mid-brown + 1 part ochre + 1 part gold + small quantity of dark brown

Oak: marble together 1 part mid-brown + 1 part dark brown + 1 part ocher

GROOVING FOR TURNED WOOD EFFECTS

This technique simulates turned wood and can be used for both miniatures and simulated wood jewelry or beads. Brass rods are available in various sizes from hobby suppliers.

YOU WILL NEED

- *Polymer clay: wood grain mixture as above*
- *Thin metal rod or fine metal knitting needle*
- *Larger knitting needle*
- *Darning needle*

1 First form the wood grain mixture into a log about ³⁄₈ in (10mm) thick and 1¹⁄₂ in (40mm) long. Be sure that all the grain is running straight down the log. Pierce through the center of the log with the metal rod and then roll it on its side on the work surface so that the log thins and lengthens along the rod. If the clay begins to pull away from the rod, simply squeeze it back on firmly and continue rolling.

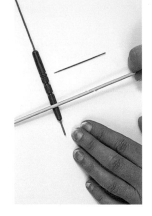

2 When the log is about ³⁄₁₆ in (5mm) thick, you are ready to 'groove' the clay. Lay a metal knitting needle across the log and saw back and forth while pressing down, causing the log and its rod to rotate on the work surface. This will make a groove all round the log. Repeat with a darning needle for a finer groove, or you can use a paintbrush handle for a wide groove. Make groups of grooves as in real wood turning.

3 The log can be baked with the rod in position to keep it straight. After baking, but while it is still warm, remove the rod and cut the grooved log to length. You can use grooved logs to make legs for miniature stools and tables. Cut out a rectangular sheet of matching wood grain for the tabletop. Glue the legs to the underside of the top using superglue.

Miniature Food

Polymer clay is the perfect material for creating miniature food for doll houses. The mixable colors, the translucent effects, the paints and powders, the addition of inclusions, the varnishes for simulating grease and wetness; all these combine to make simulating miniature food a delightful and rewarding process.

Polymer clay food techniques are also very easy for the beginner, because food rarely has

This tiny baked ham looks good enough to eat!

ROAST HAM DINNER

Roast ham with French fries and salad make a delectable miniature feast. The little ham can be sliced to make a miniature plate of food.

YOU WILL NEED

- *Polymer clay: white, red, translucent, ocher, dark brown, green, leaf green, yellow*
- *Blunt tapestry needle*
- *Small roller*
- *Artists' pastel: burnt sienna, yellow ocher, burnt umber*
- *Soft paintbrush*
- *Gloss varnish*
- *Baking parchment*

MIXTURES

- *Bone = translucent + trace of ocher*
- *Pink = 1 part red + 8 parts white*
- *Ham flesh = 1 part dark brown + 8 parts pink*
- *Fat = 1 part white + 2 parts translucent*
- *French fries = 1 part ocher + 2 parts white*

Ham bone

1 Roll a ⅛ in (3mm) thick log of bone mixture clay and cut a 1 in (25mm) length. Poke a ¼ in (6mm) hole in one end of this and bake for 10 minutes. While still warm, trim the pierced end to make the bone look cut.

2 Form a 1 in (25mm) ball of ham flesh clay and marble in a thin log of translucent clay to make it streaky. Roll out some translucent clay until it is very thin and apply this round the outside of the flesh clay. Marble a few times more to incorporate some lines of 'fat' inside the ham.

3 Shape the ham into an oval, with all the streaks running longitudinally through it. Apply more thin sheets of translucent to the outside so that it is completely covered with a thin layer. Make a hole in one end and insert the baked bone, pressing the clay tightly all round it and leaving just the cut end protruding.

an exact shape. In fact, slight irregularities will often add to the realism. The best advice is to have a photograph of the actual food beside you (or the food itself) when you make the miniature version. This will ensure that color, shape, and texture are all accurate. My favourite type of cookbook is the one with a color photograph beside every recipe—perfect for making miniature food.

Salad and french fries with cheeses to follow—made with polymer clay. The blue cheese has threads of blue-green clay running through it.

4 Make diagonal cuts all over the outside of the ham. Brush the ham with the three colors of pastel to brown it and bake the ham for 10 minutes. When it is cool, varnish with gloss varnish and cut some thin slices.

French fries
Form a ¼ in (6mm) log of the French fries mixture and roll it flat on the work surface until it is about ¹⁄₁₆ in (2mm) thick. Cut tiny strips for the French fries. Brush over them with ocher and burnt sienna pastel to brown them. Bake for 10 minutes and varnish with gloss varnish to make them look greasy.

Tomatoes
Form ³⁄₁₆ in (5mm) diameter balls of red clay. Form several ¹⁄₁₆ in (2mm) diameter balls of leaf green clay and press down on these to make flat discs. Cut V-shapes out of each disc to make them into little stars. Lay one on each red ball and poke the center of the star to make the tomato calyxes.

Lettuce
Marble together translucent clay with traces of green and yellow clay and shape into a ¼ in (6mm) thick log. Apply a thin log of translucent along one side. Cut ¹⁄₁₆ in (2mm) thick slices from the log and roll these flat on some baking parchment to prevent sticking. Curl them into leaves and bake with the tomatoes for 10 minutes.

Besides the clay itself and all the surface and inclusions materials, there are several other materials that will help your miniature food look like the real thing. Plaster of Paris or bath sealant are both useful for simulating cream. Red glass paint makes beautiful jelly in polymer clay pastry tarts. Cold casting resin or clear cold enamel are useful for simulating water or lemonade in glassware.

These sequences give only a taster of the almost endless types of miniature food that can be simulated with polymer clay. All the food shown is at 1:12 scale but you could easily adjust to make smaller scales.

Miniature cakes with a fruit flan and strawberries. The flan uses caned orange slices, while the strawberries are cream clay brushed with red artist's pastel.

SIMULATIONS AND INCLUSIONS

SPONGE CAKE WITH FEATHER ICING

This little cake is fun to make and uses yet another polymer clay technique—feathering.

YOU WILL NEED

- *Polymer clay: white, beige, golden yellow, translucent, dark brown*
- *Semolina*
- *Small dish*
- *Small roller*
- *Baking parchment*
- *Blunt tapestry needle*

MIXTURE

- *Sponge = beige + trace golden yellow*

1 Pour some semolina into the dish and mix into the sponge mixture clay. Cut open the clay to see if the semolina is well mixed in and add more until the cut surface is well speckled with semolina.

2 Form the mixture into two ⅝ in (15mm) balls and press each down onto the work surface to make two discs for the cakes, ³⁄₁₆ in (5mm) thick and about ¾ in (19mm) wide. Roll each cake on its side to straighten it. Bake the cakes for 10 minutes.

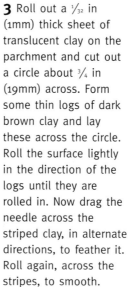

3 Roll out a ¹⁄₃₂ in (1mm) thick sheet of translucent clay on the parchment and cut out a circle about ¾ in (19mm) across. Form some thin logs of dark brown clay and lay these across the circle. Roll the surface lightly in the direction of the logs until they are rolled in. Now drag the needle across the striped clay, in alternate directions, to feather it. Roll again, across the stripes, to smooth.

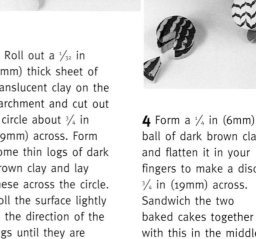

4 Form a ¼ in (6mm) ball of dark brown clay and flatten it in your fingers to make a disc ¾ in (19mm) across. Sandwich the two baked cakes together with this in the middle for the filling. Peel the feathered 'icing' off the parchment and press onto the top of the cake. Cut a slice from the cake and then bake the cake and the slice for 10 minutes. Brush some brown pastel around the sides of the cake to brown it.

PROPERTIES OF THE MAIN BRANDS OF POLYMER CLAY

The glorious colors of polymer clay give them an irresistible appeal. Color range and intensity varies considerably between the different brands.

Softness rating:
1 = soft; 5 = firm.
NB: Polymer clays harden gradually with time so this is a guide only.

Baked clay strength:
* = fragile; ***** = very strong

FIMO CLASSIC
Manufactured in Germany
Softness rating: 2-5 (currently very variable)
Number of colors: 24
Baked clay strength: ***
Smoothable? some colors
Best for: jewelry, millefiori, miniatures, flowers, and dolls (Puppenfimo soft doll clay)

FIMO SOFT
Manufactured in Germany
Softness rating: 2
Number of colors: 48
Baked clay strength: ***
Smoothable? yes
Best for: children and general hobby use

PREMO! SCULPEY
Manufactured in USA
Softness rating: 3
Number of colors: 32
Baked clay strength: ****
Gold effects? yes
Smoothable? yes
Best for: jewelry, millefiore, and all fine art techniques. Excellent artist's color range for mixing. This clay has a slightly tacky surface, and the translucent version is very translucent

SCULPEY III
Manufactured in the USA
Softness rating: 1
Number of colors: 40
Baked clay strength: *
Smoothable? yes
Best for: children and general hobby use. Baked surface has a matt quality

CERNIT
Manufactured in Germany
Softness rating: 4 (softens increasingly with hand heat)
Number of colors: 44
Baked clay strength: *****
Smoothable? no
Best for: jewelry, general hobby use, and advanced doll making (several doll clays). Porcelain effect in all colors

CREALL-THERM
Manufactured in the Netherlands
Softness rating: 4
Number of colors: 28
Baked clay strength: ***
Smoothable? yes
Best for: jewelry, millefiori, miniatures, flowers, and dolls (flesh clays). Cuts very cleanly and has a non-tacky surface

MODELLO/FORMELLO
Manufactured in Germany
Softness rating: 4
Number of colors: 24
Baked clay strength: **
Smoothable? no
Best for: general hobby use

MODELENE
Manufactured in Australia
Softness rating: 4
Number of colors: 31
Baked clay strength: *****
Smoothable? no
Best for: jewelry, miniatures, general hobby use, and advanced doll making (flesh clays)

DU-KIT
Manufactured in New Zealand
Softness rating: 4
Number of colors: 25
Baked clay strength: *****
Smoothable? yes
Best for: jewelry, miniatures, and general hobby use

FURTHER INFORMATION

SUPPLIERS

Polymer clays are widely available from art and craft materials retailers and from mail order companies. The following list includes details of mail order companies and contacts for lists of retailers. Currect information on suppliers can be found on the World Wide Web site: http://www.heaser.demon.co.uk

Australia
Staedtler (Pacific) Pty. Ltd
PO Box 576
1 Inman Road
Dee Why, NSW 2099
Tel: (00 61) 2 9982 4555
Fax: (00 61) 2 9981 2848
(For information on retailers of Fimo)

Rossdale Pty. Ltd
137 Noone Street, Clifton Hills, VIC 3068
(For information on retailers of Sculpey and Premo)

C.A.M.
197 Blackburn Road, Syndal,
VIC 3149
Tel: (00 61) 3 9802 4200
Fax: (00 61) 3 9887 9806
(For information on retailers of Modelene)

Canada
Staedtler Mars Ltd.
6 Mars Road, Etobicoke,
Ontario M9V 2K1
Tel: (001) 416 749 3966
Fax: (001) 416 745 3966
(For information on retailers of Fimo)

KJP Crafts
PO Box 5009, Merivale Depot, Nepean,
Ontario, K2C 3H3
Tel: (001) 613 225 6926
Fax: (001) 613 225 3849

New Zealand
Golding Handcrafts
PO Box 9022, Wellington
Tel/Fax: (00 64) 4 801 5855
E-mail: epdyne@compuserve.com
Website: http://www.goldingcraft.com
(Shops and mail order Du-Kit, Fimo, accessories)

Zigzag
8 Cherry Place, Casebrook, Christchurch
Tel/Fax: (00 64) 3 359 2989
E-mail: petra@zigzag.co.nz
(Mail order Sculpey, Premo, clays, tools, accessories)

United Kingdom
The Polymer Clay Pit
Meadow Rise, Wortham, Diss, Norfolk
IP22 1SQ
Tel: (00 44) 01379 646019
Fax: (00 44) 01379 646016
E-mail: claypit@heaser.demon.co.uk
Website:
http://www.heaser.demon.co.uk/claypit.htm
(Mail order Premo, Fimo, Creall-therm, powders, leafs, cutters, tissue blades, etc)

CATS Group
PO Box 12, Saxmundham, Suffolk
IP17 3PB
Tel: (00 44) 01728 648717
E-mail: CATSGroup@compuserve.com
(Mail order Cernit, some accessories)

Homecrafts Direct
PO Box 247 Leicester LE1 9QS
Tel: (00 44) 0116 251 0405
Fax: (00 44) 0116 251 5015
E-mail: post@speccrafts.demon.co.uk
Website:
http://www.speccrafts.demon.co.uk
(Mail order Formello, tools, accessories, cold enamels)

USA
Clay Factory of Escondido
PO Box 460598
Escondido
CA 92046-0598
Tel: (001) 760 741 3242
Fax: (001) 760 741 5436
E-mail: clayfactoryinc@clayfactoryinc.com
Website: http://www.clayfactoryinc.com
(Shop and mail order Cernit, Sculpey, Premo, tools, cutters, accessories)

Polymer Clay Express
25-5 Broad Street, suite 242, Freehold
NJ 07728
Tel: (001) 732 431 1390
Fax: (001) 732 431 2986
E-mail: Polyexp@polymerclayexpress.com
(Mail order Fimo, Cernit, Premo, Sculpey III, tools, accessories)

Rio Grande
7500 Bluewater Road NW
Albuquerque, NM 87121-1962
Tel: 1 800 545 6566
Fax: 1 800 965 2329
E-mail: bluegem@riogrande.com
Website: http://www.riogrande.com
(Mail order Cernit, leafs, accessories and cold (epoxy) enamels)

POLYMER CLAY ORGANISATIONS

Please send a stamped addressed envelope when enquiring about membership.

The British Polymer Clay Guild
Meadow Rise, Wortham, Diss, Norfolk
IP22 1SQ, UK

The National Polymer Clay Guild
Suite 115-345, 1350 Beverly Road,
McLean, VA 22101, USA

FURTHER READING

Carlson, Maureen,
How to Make Clay Characters
(North Light Books, Cincinnati, Ohio 1997)

Ford, Steven and Dierks, Leslie
Creating With Polymer Clay: Design, Techniques and Projects
(Lark Books, Asheville, N Carolina 1996)

Heaser, Sue
Making Polymer Clay Jewellery
(Cassell, London 1997)

Heaser, Sue
Making Doll's House Miniatures with Polymer Clay
(Ward Lock, London 1997)

Heaser, Sue
Making Miniature Dolls with Polymer Clay
(Ward Lock, London 1999)

Kato, Donna
The Art of Polymer Clay
(Watson Guptill, New York 1997)

Roche, Nan
The New Clay
(Flower Valley Press, Rockville, Maryland 1991)

Thompson, Suzann
The Polymer Clay Sourcebook
(Hamlyn, London 1999)

Quast, Barbara
Making Miniature Flowers with Polymer Clay
(North Light Books, Cincinnati, Ohio, 1998)

INDEX

128

ACKNOWLEDGMENTS

I have tried to be as meticulous as possible in acknowledging the inventors of various techniques in this book. If a technique is unacknowledged, it was either developed by me or is of such a universal nature that to suggest a single inventor would be unrealistic. I would particularly like to thank Gwen Gibson, Mike Buesseler, and Pier Voulkos who so generously described their wonderful discoveries to me.

The Heron project on pages 83 to 85 was designed and demonstrated by Alexandra Blythe, who specialises in natural history miniatures and accepts commissions. She can be contacted at:

Four Seasons Miniatures, 48 Park Close, Hethersett, Norwich, Norfolk. NR9 3EW U.K. Tel: (00 44) 01603 810346.

Quarto would like to acknowledge and thank the following for providing pictures used in this book. While every effort has been made to acknowledge copyright holders we would like to apologize should there have been any omissions. The author would also like to thank these artists for their enthusiastic contributions to the project:

Christine Alibert; Jody Bishel; Alexandra Blythe; Mike Buesseler; Carol Bull;
Katherine Dewey; Diane Dunville; Gwen Gibson; Linda Goff; Maria Gower;
Amelia Helm; Akiko Kase; Donna Kato; Patricia Kimle; Kazuyo Kono;
Karen Lewis; Patricia Robison; Sylvia Schmahmann; Hen Scott; Marie Segal;
Lynda Struble; Pier Voulkos and Daniel Peters.

Credits for photography:
James Clay Walls p. 72 right; Michael-Leonard Creditor p. 27 bottom and p 100 top left; George Post p. 26 top left; Dixon Withers-Julian p 26 bottom left.
All other photographs are the copyright of Quarto.